POLICY AND PRACTICE IN EDUCATION

NUMBER NINETEEN

BUILDING A LEARNING COMMUNITY
IN THE PRIMARY CLASSROOM

POLICY AND PRACTICE IN EDUCATION

POLICY AND PRACTICE IN EDUCATION

SERIES EDITORS
JIM O'BRIEN and CHRISTINE FORDE

BUILDING A LEARNING COMMUNITY IN THE PRIMARY CLASSROOM

Margaret Martin

*Lecturer in Educational Studies,
University of Glasgow*

DUNEDIN ACADEMIC PRESS
EDINBURGH

Published by
Dunedin Academic Press Ltd
Hudson House
8 Albany Street
Edinburgh EH1 3QB
Scotland

ISBN: 978-1-903765-68-5
ISSN 1479-6910

British Library Cataloguing in Publication data
A catalogue record for this book is available from the British Library

Typeset by Makar Publishing Production
Printed in Great Britain by Cromwell Press

CONTENTS

SERIES EDITORS' INTRODUCTION

In the first decade of the new millennium certain trends in education and schooling are discernible on a global scale. There are emphases on standards associated with student achievement; on professional renewal allied to school cultural change; and on curriculum development leading to more personal learning and skill development for school students.

In this book, Margaret Martin considers what she believes to be the most effective ways to organise learning in primary schools. Her views are informed by her understanding of the theoretical literature and allied to her grounded experience as a teacher, head teacher, adviser and researcher/consultant. She unashamedly promotes the concept of a 'learning community' as being the way forward. The primary school is a key area for child development. Traditionally there has been more opportunity for individual expression by primary teachers. They have applied their professional judgement in terms of curriculum and in teaching methodology, especially in relation to more child-centred education. Martin concedes that in the later decades of the twentieth century this freedom has been under attack in several systems. However, she suggests that there is now a greater appreciation of teaching and learning processes and a reaction against over-prescription. This book offers an analysis of the issues associated with developing creativity and critical skills in students and offers grounded examples of how to build and sustain learning communities which will foster such development. The consideration afforded to associated issues of teacher pedagogy, professional development and specific classroom approaches includes a review of specific named initiatives. The author invites practitioners and policy makers to reflect on their own particular contexts and then to assess whether co-operative learning as endorsed should be supported.

Dr Jim O'Brien
Vice Dean and Director,
Centre for Educational Leadership,
Moray House School of Education,
The University of Edinburgh

Dr Christine Forde
Senior Lecturer in Educational Studies
The University of Glasgow

INTRODUCTION

In this book I argue that the most effective way to organise learning in the primary classroom is through the creation of a learning community. Co-operative learning is proposed as the best vehicle for creating this collaborative environment and, therefore, should be at the core of a teacher's repertoire of teaching skills. A learning community does not just 'happen': it has to be consciously and consistently developed and nurtured by the teacher, through the use of specific strategies to promote collaboration and participation.

In Chapter 2, the case is made for co-operative, interactive learning using the sound theoretical and research base to be found in the literature. For some teachers, this will be the chapter they find least attractive. Much has been written about teachers and their relationship with theory: I want to lay my cards on the table. I believe my own practice over the past five years has improved considerably as result of research into co-operative learning and formative assessment. The evidence is very persuasive and has provided me with an informed rationale for my practice. Practical training and on-going discussion and reflection with colleagues has also been influential. In our work with postgraduate student teachers at the University of Glasgow, we need to persuade students that the approaches we are advocating are valid: the research provides that rationale. Teachers may also want to be in a position to justify their choice of teaching methods and there is no better source than the literature in the field. I urge teachers to read this chapter, even if they come back to it after they have read the other chapters.

Chapter 3 addresses the crucial importance of the teacher's mindset in determining commitment to a particular way of teaching. Teachers need to be convinced of its value and its benefits for learners, so, in addition to examining the political and theoretical context, and the technical expertise required, the role of personal and professional values and beliefs in the choices teachers make about organising learning will also be examined. Many of these choices are based upon unexamined assumptions and 'commonsense' views of teaching and learning. I am challenging teachers to identify and explore the personal stance that informs their practice in the classroom. The personal dimension of teaching cannot be ignored if there is to be any real chance of persuading teachers to alter radically their approaches in the classroom and they need the time and space to reflect on their own individual reactions as they move from one methodology to another. This is best done with colleagues where possible to share concerns and successes.

In Chapter 4, the key components of a learning community in action in the classroom are outlined. I suggest some co-operative learning strategies that might be used and recommend appropriate sources to allow readers to find out much more than this short book permits.

If there is to be any significant change in our classrooms, the support and training available to students and teachers alike needs to be focused and relevant. In Chapter 5, recommendations are made for Initial Teacher Education and teachers' Continuing Professional Development.

But to begin with, in Chapter 1 this collaborative approach to teaching is set in a wider context. I believe that we have never been so well placed to make a real difference to the way we organise the learning in Scottish classrooms. The prevailing policy context provides a favourable backdrop for the changes to methodology advocated in this book, and the time is right to grasp the opportunity.

Chapter 1

THE POLICY CONTEXT

To set the scene, it is useful to track the developing policy context of Scottish education and the ways in which that may be impacting on the ability of teachers to build real learning communities in their classrooms. Just as our traditionalism in Scotland saved us from the worst excesses of 'progressive education', our egalitarianism will allow us to seize the opportunities presented by A Curriculum for Excellence (SEED, 2004) to change the way we approach primary education. The Primary Memorandum (1965) has never looked more attractive. Informed by a new rigour, brought about by years of increasing accountability, and a renewed focus on formative assessment, we have the building blocks to create high quality, genuinely learner-centred education.

Child-centred approaches

In the last ten years there has been a shift in the policy agenda, marked by a new focus on the quality of learning and teaching in the classroom, much of it informed by an increased understanding of the ways in which children learn and how they can be best supported in their learning. This move from content to process, has been largely welcomed by Scottish teachers in the primary sector, where it is seen by many, as an opportunity to return to what they perceive to be 'good teaching' associated with developments such as the Primary Memorandum (SOED, 1965) and the Plowden Report (Central Advisory Council for Education, 1967). These focused on active learning and child-centred approaches set in a quite different political context. It is interesting to speculate on the reasons why these approaches, so acceptable at the time, became so out of step with the policy agenda of the 1980s and 1990s, and have gained renewed respectability in the early twenty-first century.

The 1960s were characterised by post-war liberal optimism. Resources were plentiful and the emphasis was on the role of education as the solution to social problems and the way to build a better society for the second half of the twentieth century. In terms of methodology, approaches to learning and teaching were based on research into child development and, in particular, the work of Piaget. Teachers were advised to follow the interests of the child, be flexible in their teaching, and make learning meaningful for children by integrating the subject elements of the curriculum. Tests were seen as unhelpful and of limited value. Indeed the Memorandum went so far as to say that they should 'not assume undue importance in the work of the school, or impose an undesirable rigidity on curriculum and methods' (SOED, 1965, p. 49). This would be music to the ears of teachers in twenty-first century Scotland.

Curriculum-centred approaches

Major changes came with the Thatcher governments from 1979 onwards, which affected the structure of schooling in Scotland irrevocably. The Self-Governing Schools etc. (Scotland) Act (1989) introduced Devolved School Management: parents were offered the chance to become involved in the management of schools through the School Board (Scotland) Act 1988. The 1981 Education (Scotland) Act opened the door to a market model with the introduction of parental choice of school and information to help parents choose between schools was to become available through the introduction of national testing (SOED, 1992) and, eventually, published examination results. These key changes impacted on practice in the primary sector. The market model was increasingly applied as education was reconceptualised as a 'product', the 'consumers' being the pupils and parents. A new group of consumers (parents) was introduced into the decision-making process, and teachers, schools and local authorities were to be held increasingly accountable for the service delivered. The idea behind these changes was that standards would be driven up as competition between schools exposed poor performance and schools would be publicly judged by their results.

The outcome of these developments was that policy makers began to focus on the prescription of curriculum content for Scottish schools, like their counterparts in the rest of the UK. The introduction of the 5–14 curriculum guidelines in the early 1990s signalled direct government intervention in the learning process. Despite having avoided some of the worst excesses of the very prescriptive nature of the National Curriculum in England, Scottish teachers still felt constrained by the introduction of an increasingly rigid framework of curriculum content and an imposed assessment structure. There can be no doubt that the average primary teacher in Scotland saw this as a huge restriction on their ability to be spontaneous and responsive in their teaching. Many teachers saw the need to account for every detail of every minute of the day as genuinely limiting their capacity to find the time to interact with children as individuals. Teachers have questioned the idea that children are empty vessels waiting to be 'filled up' with 5–14, and argued that learning is much messier than the seductive neatness and linear progression of the curriculum guidelines.

In their study of English primary teachers' responses to the introduction of the national curriculum, Osborne *et al.* found much disturbing evidence:

> The pressures from a restricted but overloaded national curriculum, combined with 'high stakes' national testing, appears to be diminishing the opportunities for teachers to work in a way that enables them to 'develop the whole child' and address the social concerns of society.
>
> (Osborne *et al.*, 2000, p. 160)

I argue strongly that these conditions did not and will not support an effective learning community. The creation of a community of learners requires space for building community and working in that very affective domain, which is squeezed as teachers are held accountable for 'covering the curriculum'. The process of learning is reduced to a technical activity, time limited and compartmentalised. The opportunities to connect up the learning are fewer, as heavy emphasis is laid on performance in individual subject areas as evidenced by the increased use of setting in primary school classrooms in an effort for schools to meet performance targets. The resulting labelling of children is a concern for those viewing diversity as a strength, rather than a weakness. These approaches are divisive and at odds with the idea of creating learning community in the classroom. Griffith dismisses curriculum prescription as disastrous:

> the National Curriculum . . . effectively demands that 11 years of state education are devoted to learning by heart bits of 'knowledge' that can be examined by written tests of memory, and the school-leaving cohort graded from A–G.
>
> (Griffith, 2000, p. 201)

Learning-centred approaches

Today, the context is considerably different. Education has moved through the New Right policies of the Thatcher years, which culminated in the prescription of curriculum content as described above, to the New Labour policies of the last nine years. The drive to raise attainment and improve performance is still paramount, but the focus has shifted towards education for all and a social inclusion agenda. This has been translated into education agendas which focus on how teachers teach, rather than what they teach. Our increasing understanding of learning styles (Kolb, 1984; Entwistle, 1988; Bayne, 1995) and multiple intelligences (Gardner, 1983) has concentrated attention on the ways in which children make sense of the teaching they experience in school and the strategies that teachers might use to support them. The creation of the Scottish Parliament has allowed the opportunity for Scotland to develop its own approaches to education in an even more distinctive fashion than was possible before 1998. A number of key policies have been put in place which have helped set the scene for the changing face of Scottish education, and I have chosen to focus on what I believe to be the two most influential initiatives:

- A Curriculum for Excellence (2004)
- Assessment is for Learning (2002)

The first provides a framework which legitimises the idea that we need to reorganise the ways in which learning takes place; the second provides the practical strategies, based on extensive research, and supported by significant investment in staff development, which teachers can use to effect that change.

A Curriculum for Excellence

A Curriculum for Excellence (ACE) lays out a clear set of values and purposes for education in Scotland from 3 to 18. The seven principles of curriculum design detailed there have some resonance with the approaches to learning and teaching advocated in this book: challenge and enjoyment, breadth, progression, depth, personalisation and choice, coherence and relevance, and these will be explored in greater depth in subsequent chapters. The impetus to update the curriculum came from the National Debate in Scotland (2000). It recognised that, although there was satisfaction with some elements of the Scottish curriculum, the changing context of the twenty-first century demanded a different approach. 'Our aspiration is to enable all children to develop their capacities as successful learners, confident individuals, responsible citizens and effective contributors to society' (SEED, 2004).

Too often in primary schools, children are all busy doing work of little challenge or interest, for which they can see no real life relevance and over which they have no choice or control. If we are to fulfil the aims of ACE, there needs to be greater emphasis on making meaning and connection in the work that children do, and teachers need to spend more time helping children make sense of new learning. The retention of knowledge and understanding is central to learning and children need to be engaged actively within relevant, meaningful contexts.

In addition to the four capacities to be developed as part of A Curriculum for Excellence –

- successful learners
- confident individuals
- responsible citizens
- effective contributors

– the Scottish Executive Education Department (SEED) identified three factors integral to the development of these capacities:

- the environment for learning;
- the choice of teaching and learning approaches;
- the ways in which learning is organised.

These three factors lead directly into questions about the kind of class-room communities we create and how we conduct the day-to-day business of teaching and learning in Scottish schools. ACE encourages teachers to make learning active and to give children opportunities to develop and demonstrate their creativity. The ACE framework urges teachers and schools to examine their teaching practices critically and consider their effectiveness. How fit for purpose are they in delivering the four capacities? The high stakes accountability of the last twenty years has pushed teachers further and further towards 'covering the curriculum', often at the cost of the very flexibility and creativity now being advocated. ACE gives teachers the opportunity to reclaim that ground. This is exciting, but may be challenging for those who have lost some of their skills in organising more learner-centred education, or who have never had the opportunity to develop them.

Informed and responsible citizenship does not follow from predominantly teacher-directed activity, where children's main aim becomes to please the teacher: it comes from learning environments where children are encouraged to think for themselves and take some responsibility for their own learning and their own behaviour. This requires a different approach to learning and teaching that encourages independent and interdependent learners.

While there is still a concern for academic attainment, teachers are now also being encouraged to consider the wider range of skills and qualities that will be required to meet the challenges of the twenty-first century. The approach to learning and teaching proposed in this book fits hand in glove with these aspirations of A Curriculum for Excellence; indeed, I argue that there are few other approaches which could deliver these SEED requirements more effectively. A Curriculum for Excellence emphasises the importance of ensuring that assessment supports effective learning. This is at the heart of effective teaching and learning and is the reason for the choice of the Assessment is for Learning programme as the second influential policy context for this book.

Assessment is for Learning

Scotland's approach to assessment had been clearly laid out in *Guidelines for Assessment 5-14* (SOED, 1991), where teachers were urged to use assessment as a tool to inform teaching. Hutchison and Hayward (2005) point to the particular context at that time which affected the uptake of this guidance. At the same time as *Guidelines for Assessment 5–14* was published, the 5–14 guidelines on Mathematics and Language were also introduced. The profession naturally focused on the implementation of the basic curricular guidelines in an atmosphere of increasing pressure to measure attainment. National testing was introduced shortly afterwards and the emphasis on high stakes summative assessment became firmly established. Because the assessment guidance was published separately from the curriculum guidance, a clear message was also sent to teachers that the two things were unconnected and should be addressed separately. In many ways an early opportunity to move into genuinely formative assessment practices was missed at this time.

The *Review of Assessment in Pre-School and 5–14* (SEED, 1999), established the Assessment Development Programme. The review gave an important place to formative assessment and was very much influenced by the work of Black and Wiliam (1998a, 1998b), which made explicit links between formative assessment and raising attainment. The Assessment is for Learning (AifL) programme was introduced in 2002 and marked the beginnings of a stronger link between assessment and the promotion of learning. It had gained support on the back of the shifting priorities in Scottish education, arising out of the National Debate and the resulting National Priorities established in 2000 (see SEED, 2000). Scottish teachers and parents had never been comfortable with an over-emphasis on summative assessment in the primary sector. Their resistance to the introduction of National Testing in 1991 is clear evidence of this e.g. 85% of Glasgow parents withdrew their children from National Testing. (Paterson, 2003) The research that has taken place in the interim, and informed the AifL initiative, has provided the impetus for a gradual shift in practice in Scottish primary school classrooms. The relationship between policy, practice and research has never been stronger, in sharp contrast to the absence of the research base in the early 1990s. As long ago as 1993, Black was warning of the nature of the real shift that would need to be made:

> To incorporate formative assessment into their teaching would involve teachers in much more than the acquisition of the necessary skills. Their view of the teaching of their own subject might have to change if they are to be close to their students in guiding them. The changes in their classroom practice might also involve profound changes of role, even for teachers regarded by themselves and others as highly successful.
>
> (Black, 1993, p. 79)

The key features of AifL that impact directly on classroom practice relate to the ways in which teachers engage with children: sharing learning intentions, identifying clear success criteria, providing opportunities for self and peer assessment, and giving effective feedback.

There is a strong focus on *sharing the learning intentions*, so that the learners are very clear about what they are learning and why. This may seem an obvious and easy change in practice, but it is a complex matter for teachers to identify in detail, the aims for each lesson. The recent emphasis on curriculum coverage has led many teachers to be concerned with working their way through published resources and their planning can often reflect that imperative. AifL has encouraged teachers to think very carefully about learning intentions and ways of sharing them meaningfully with the children in their classes.

These learning intentions should be accompanied by *success criteria*, written in child-friendly language so that children are very clear about what is expected of them and what steps they might take to get there. This is an even more demanding requirement of teachers, who have to break the learning down into manageable chunks, which the children can then use to help them achieve the learning intention. These success criteria serve two main purposes: to support the learners in making their way to the learning intention and to provide a useful focus for self, peer and teacher assessment. The development of appropriate success criteria is an important part of the teaching process, and children should be involved in their generation as they work with the teacher to identify the key elements of the learning.

Self and *peer assessment* are important dimensions of formative assessment. Children are encouraged to use success criteria to examine critically their own and each other's work. This shift in responsibility is an important change in the relationship between learners and teacher and a key feature of formative assessment. It allows children to work in collaboration with peers to enhance their learning and use the skills and strengths of the other children in the class.

The importance of *effective feedback* is highlighted in AifL and teachers are given detailed advice on the nature of feedback designed to support learning and help children identify the steps required to close the gap between their current and desired performance.

All of the above require the children to engage in an active way with their learning and to become much more aware of the purpose and relevance of the work they do in school. This means the teacher has to develop a teaching style which encourages participation and engagement, with much less emphasis on written exercises and worksheets. The skill of effective questioning is also highlighted and the ways in which teachers can encourage the participation of larger numbers of children in the class. These different dimensions of formative assessment, which relate to teaching in the classroom, add up to a considerable change in practice for some teachers. For others, they provide structure and rigour to elements of good teaching with which many teachers are already familiar.

Simpson details the conditions which need to be met if teachers are to engage with formative assessment:

- New strategies need to be clearly explained in straightforward, non technical language.
- The changes must be seen by teachers to be problem-solving.
- Models need to be provided so that teachers are clear about what's required.
- They need to understand the underlying principles which inform the strategies.

(Simpson, 2003, p. 725)

Black and Wiliam (1998a, 1998b) advocate the kind of staff development opportunities which lead to depth of understanding in formative assessment and this is a major step forward from the cascade model of the 1980s and 1990s, where staff were sent to centrally organised in-service training courses with the expectation that they would feed back their new knowledge and skills to their colleagues in school. There were flaws in this model since the majority of teachers experienced the training 'second hand' and gained much less as a result.

A considerable amount of support has been available to promote formative assessment in Scotland during the last twenty years, laying a sound foundation for what was to come. The AifL initiative, however, with its extensive research base, investment of resources and staff development programme, has gone a long way to meeting Simpson's conditions and this may account partly for its success in Scottish primary schools. A collaborative approach has been used, involving all major stakeholders: local and national policy makers, Learning and Teaching Scotland (LTS), Her Majesty's Inspectorate of Education (HMIE), the Scottish Qualifications Authority (SQA), teachers' professional organisations, researchers, parents and teachers. This building of a collaborative approach was informed by research and past experience, and has led to the establishment of effective support structures to encourage implementation.

Teachers have welcomed the detailed exploration of the ways in which children's learning can be enhanced by the use of rigorous formative assessment strategies. This approach may indeed appeal to the relatively conservative, but essentially learner-centred approach of Scottish primary teachers, who prefer rigour in their child-centredness. Interestingly, rather than focusing exclusively on assessment practices, this initiative has impacted quite dramatically on the day-to-day teaching repertoire of primary school teachers. Staff development programmes in local authorities and individual schools, as well as a range of support material, has meant that teachers have been exposed to formative assessment strategies and have begun experimenting in the classroom. Many have found themselves to be comfortable with the new strategies, recognising them as 'just good teaching'.

The current emphasis on formative assessment has evolved in Scotland over a twenty-year period and has now reached a critical stage where large numbers of primary school teachers are willing to engage with the ideas and the practical strategies being recommended. The blend of influences described by Simpson above, mean that the chances of sustained interest are relatively high. What is not so clear is whether the implementation is at a technical level only, or whether teachers are engaging at a deeper level of understanding the philosophy underpinning these techniques.

Evaluations are encouraging:

> Teachers have frequently made reference to evidence of deeper learning amongst their students and noted the particular impact on children who find learning hard. Moreover there is substantial evidence of similar increases in engagement, confidence, and enthusiasm on the part of the teachers in the project.
>
> (Hayward *et al.*, 2004, p. 411)

In their evaluation of Project 1 of the Assessment is for Learning Development Programme: Support for Professional Practice in Formative Assessment, Hallam *et al.* (2004) found that the level of teachers' engagement was 'very powerful' and that practice had been successfully changed. Motivation, enthusiasm and commitment to the project were positively affected. They found this to be one of the most positive outcomes of the project. They described the changes in teachers in these terms:

- better informed
- engaged with the literature
- considered their practice critically
- reported deeper understanding of the learning process
- believed they could improve the learning in their classrooms
- renewed confidence about learning.

Possibly most significantly, they reported a shift in the power relationships between teachers and children, teachers 'being more prepared to relax control and empower their pupils' (Hallam *et al.*, 2004, p. 133).

> For several projects, an implicit if not explicit aim was to change practice in classrooms in quite significant ways. For practitioners this can be challenging, if not threatening, but overall there was strong agreement from headteachers and teachers that being involved in AifL had led to changed practices. There was evidence that achieving change had been challenging, indicating the extent to which teachers' existing beliefs about assessment (and how children learn) were being questioned.
>
> (Condie *et al.*, 2005, p. 145)

There would seem to be cause for cautious optimism.

National initiatives: a good or a bad thing?

It is possible to view these current trends as the 'meddling' of government in the teaching practices of professional, qualified teachers. On the other hand, it is also possible that these initiatives have had a considerable positive impact already in Scottish schools, influencing the quality of teaching and learning in many primary school classrooms.

The *what* of teaching is the easy part: the *how*, and more importantly, the *why*, are much more complex and challenging. Both are addressed in this book as we explore the ways in which effective co-operative learning supports a successful learning community. If Scottish teachers have begun to change their practices, why is that the case? Why is it that the current focus on teaching strategies and the ways in which children learn have caught the imagination of many Scottish primary school teachers? What have been the influencing factors on their decisions about changing their approaches to teaching? Are they just technical changes or changes of heart? Why are some reluctant to change?

It is often the case that, despite the best intentions of government and local authorities in introducing new initiatives, teachers resolutely remain unchanged in their practice. The gulf between the policy and the actual practice in classrooms can be enormous. Policy changes which relate to teaching strategies, and which require teachers to 'buy in' to the philosophy being promoted, are even more likely to falter, since they involve a change of mindset on the part of the teacher. Because teaching is a deeply personal activity, involving beliefs and values about learners and learning, about teachers and teaching, it is not simply a matter of providing guidelines and staff development opportunities. It is also about winning hearts and minds.

The change of mindset required to move to the creation of a real learning community in the classroom is more than a change in instructional strategies; for some teachers, it is a change of philosophy. That change in philosophy can be made easier, or more difficult, by the prevailing policy context and in Scotland in the early twenty-first century, we are well placed to capitalise on the momentum provided by A Curriculum for Excellence. Equally helpful is the introduction of high profile support for formative assessment practices, through the Assessment is for Learning programme, which focuses attention on the changing role of the teacher and her relationship with the children in her class.

The notion of a community of learners is an essentially democratic, egalitarian approach to teaching, which puts the learner at the centre and necessarily alters the balance of power and control in the classroom. Learners in such a classroom are increasingly expected to take responsibility for their own learning and to become involved in some decision-making. They are encouraged to question and investigate, rather than accept passively the teacher's words of wisdom. For many teachers this is in direct opposition to their beliefs about the teacher–learner relationship and their rights and responsibilities. Even for those whose value system is not at odds with this approach to learning, the changed relationship can still feel like jumping off a cliff. The move from being the 'sage on the stage' to genuine facilitation of learning is not easy for most teachers. This dilemma is explored further in Chapter 2.

Chapter 2

TURNING THEORY INTO PRACTICE

This chapter focuses on the research base and practical implications of the developing policy agenda outlined in Chapter 1. It challenges the prevailing transmission model of teaching and learning and advocates a more constructivist approach to learning in the primary classroom with active involvement of pupils and teacher, while recognising the inherent tensions created in the classroom as a result of changing curriculum and assessment imperatives.

A Curriculum for Excellence sets an agenda for teachers which encourages them to reflect upon their practice and the extent to which it will deliver successful learners, confident individuals, effective contributors and responsible citizens. The Assessment is for Learning initiative has addressed the issue of changing practices in the classroom in some detail, giving extensive advice to teachers about teaching and learning strategies. But how does this advice sit with current and developing practice in the classroom?

The transmission model of learning

Probably the most common instructional strategy in Scottish schools is the transmission model, where the teacher does the talking and the children do the listening. It could be described as teacher centred. The teacher is traditionally positioned at the front, doing the teaching and choosing children to answer questions. If teaching were the same as 'telling' it would be easy for children to learn, but we know it is much more complex than that. However teachers still feel compelled to fill the space and often do not feel they are earning their money if they do not do all the talking, all the explaining, all the drawing conclusions, all the thinking out loud. Palmer (1998) asks teachers to spend less time filling the space with information and their own thoughts and more time opening up a space where children can engage in dialogue with the ideas and each other. He encourages teachers not to listen to that voice inside their heads that says they should be filling the space to justify themselves, but acknowledges that it does take much more skill and confidence to open up a learning space than to fill it. The confidence of many Scottish teachers has been gradually eroded by the rapid pace of change, and the increase in accountability (Osborne *et al.*, 2000; Ward, 2004; Mahoney *et al.*, 2004), so it is easy to understand why they might revert to what they know best, what they feel most comfortable with, and what they feel best serves the children: teaching from the front, where many primary teachers have considerable skills. Add to this the raising attainment agenda, particularly in relation to literacy and numeracy, which encourages more whole-class teaching, and the path to traditional, teacher-centred approaches is clearly laid out. These imperatives may be applied less stringently in Scotland than in England and Wales, but the underlying philosophy is very similar and the possible effects on teachers' perceptions of what constitutes 'effective teaching' are worthy of consideration (Mahoney *et al.*, 2004).

The transmission model of learning is essentially about the acquisition of knowledge and the memorisation and reproduction of content. Because the learners are such passive recipients in the process, they become highly dependent on the teacher as the holder of knowledge and arbiter of all that goes on in the classroom. The result is children who are unlikely to develop important independent learning and self-evaluation skills or any real depth of understanding of new learning. Ironically, the ability to reproduce content, so highly valued in this model, is only a very short-term benefit.

The commonly used diagram below shows the retention rates for various instructional strategies (adapted from Craigen and Ward, 1999).

Figure 2.1 Learning Pyramid – % Average Retention Rate

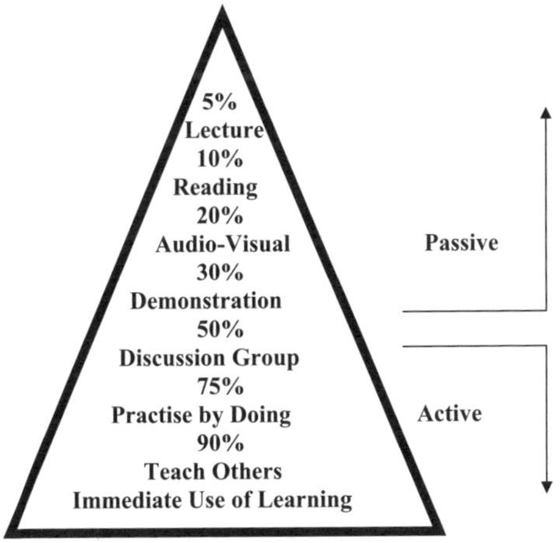

5%
Lecture
10%
Reading
20%
Audio-Visual
30%
Demonstration
50%
Discussion Group
75%
Practise by Doing
90%
Teach Others
Immediate Use of Learning

Passive

Active

(adapted from Craigen and Ward 1999)

It demonstrates what is almost self-evident: the more actively involved the learner becomes in the learning, the more likely it is that new learning will be retained. The opportunity to practise new skills and perform new understanding embeds learning in a more effective way than when the learner is a passive recipient of new knowledge.

Setting

Another common response to the raising attainment agenda and resulting imperative to get through more and more curricular content is the increasing use of setting in the primary school. It is now common to find children assigned to ability groups, mostly for mathematics and language, and often across class stages, in order to create a smaller, more manageable number of working groups for allocation to teachers. This setting typically takes place at a given time, usually in the morning, when children will move into the assigned groups, often in different classrooms, and has to be strictly timetabled. Although the use of IQ as a mechanism for selection has been largely discredited, we still rely on ability groupings as a solution to raising attainment in schools. Increased stress on accountability mean it is not surprising that teachers follow the path laid down by government and inspectors towards increased attainment through setting according to ability levels. This labelling of children at an increasingly earlier age is not helpful to their view of themselves as effective learners. We don't now send them to different schools, in separate locations, but do we make sure they are just as aware of their ability through the grouping of pupils within one school. We do this now at a much earlier age.

The purpose seems to be mainly about raising attainment, usually as measured by tests, usually in a narrow range of subjects. However, the focus is on surface and strategic learning of the most superficial kind, designed to achieve the desired results in the short term. The longer term, deeper learning for understanding seems to be much less important. This approach is based on the questionable notions that:

- It is possible to accurately measure ability in a neutral and value-free way.
- These narrow measures of ability continue to apply over time and across intelligences.
- We have chosen the 'right' chunks of knowledge and understanding for children to learn at school.
- Sorting children by ability will lead to more effective learning.
- Testing is the best way to check learning.
- Academic intelligence is more important than all the others.

(Gilborn and Youdell, 2001)

Is it possible to draw sensible conclusions about a child's ability from their performance in a particular test? And then, working from those conclusions, should we proceed to allocate time, resources, and most important of all, expectations? We then act on our assumptions as though testing was an exact science that was value-free and unconnected to the human dimension of learning. Objections to this arrangement relate to what makes for effective learning. Children who think they are stupid are unlikely to be in a position to capitalise on the learning opportunities in the classroom. They are more likely to switch off, to find coping strategies to deal with the system they're in, to cause disruption, to disengage from learning generally. Objections also relate to the feelings of those children who are relegated to the bottom of the pile at some stage in their school career. The following poem powerfully illustrates the point:

Slow Reader

I – am – in – the – slow –
read – ers – group – my – broth
er – is – in – the – foot
ball – team – my – sis – ter
is – a – ser – ver – my
lit – tle – broth – er – was
a – wise – man – in – the
in – fants – christ – mas – play
I – am – in – the – slow
read – ers – group – that – is
all – I – am – in – I
hate – it

from PLEASE MRS BUTLER
by Allan Ahlberg (Kestrel, 1983) © Allan Ahlberg, 1983.
Reproduced by kind permission.

Dividing children up into ability groups is not necessarily the most effective way to organise learning.

Transformation model of learning

Teaching for Effective Learning (1996), published by the Scottish Consultative Council on the Curriculum (SCCC), was an important document in Scotland. It pulled together much of the research evidence which was emerging at that time about learning and teaching, presented it in an accessible format, and contributed to the developing discourse focused on pedagogy, rather than curriculum content. The following are some of the key ideas highlighted in this document that were influential in opening up the debate about the nature of effective learning:

- Intelligence is not fixed.
- There is no such thing as a single general intelligence, which we all possess to a greater or lesser degree.

- Learning involves developing our emotions and feelings along with our ability to think and act.
- We are more likely to learn when we are motivated to do so. Young people who feel good about themselves are much more likely to be highly motivated to learn.
- We learn most effectively when we think things through for ourselves.
- Learning is messy. We rarely learn anything by proceeding along a single path to predetermined outcomes.
- Most learning involves other people.
- Self-awareness, including awareness of ourselves as learners, helps us learn more effectively.
- We can learn how to learn by developing skills which help us think, feel and act more effectively.

Each of these statements points to a part of the jigsaw of transformational learning. They challenge the transmission model of learning outlined above and offer an alternative perspective. The transformation model of learning is the one that offers most opportunity for the implementation of A Curriculum for Excellence and sits comfortably with possibility of building a learning community in the classroom.

The transformation model of learning is grounded in theories of the central importance of experience in learning, most notably put forward by John Dewey (1963), which argue the case that the learner's experience should be the obvious starting-point for other learning. Boud and Miller (1996) argue five key propositions about learning from experience:

- Experience is the foundation of, and stimulus for, learning. It is a central consideration and cannot be bypassed.
- Learners actively construct their own experience, influenced by their unique past, as well as current context.
- Learning is holistic and the connectedness of knowledge must be highlighted.
- Learning is socially and culturally constructed and it is challenging to move beyond the influence of context and culture.
- Learning is influenced by the socio-emotional context in which it occurs.

They sum it up thus: 'Learning is an act of becoming aware of experience, building upon it, extending it and in the process, creating new experiences which become part of what we know' (Boud and Miller, 1996, p. 8).

This is an important reminder to teachers that the agenda for learning should not be theirs exclusively and that they ignore the reality of the learners in front of them at their peril. This is difficult for some teachers to accept, given their own past learning experiences in school and in university, and given the resource-driven, de-contextualised nature of much of the teaching which now takes place in Scottish classrooms. The teacher needs to be concerned about the children's interests and skills, using them to motivate and encourage learning. This is possible in the primary school classroom, where teachers work consistently with the same group of children, over a long period of time, and come to know them exceptionally well. This model of learning demands that teachers value their own depth of knowledge and use it to best effect in organising effective, relevant learning for children. The emotional dimension of learning is also important and has to be addressed in the environment created by teachers. This aspect of the learning environment will be dealt with in Chapter 4.

Constructivism

Constructivist theories of learning have increased our understanding of how children learn from one another. The constructivist classroom is where the transformation model is most likely to flourish. Both from a social and personal constructivist viewpoint, the importance of social interaction in promoting learning and thinking is generally acknowledged. Vygotsky (1978) argues that interaction with more able adults or peers, to mediate the learning was effective. Social construction of new understandings, knowledge and skills is encouraged through opportunities to model skills and receive feedback. The requirement to justify and explain thinking leads to a deeper understanding. Piaget (1932) argues that cognitive conflict is a catalyst for change where the learner reassesses understandings and constructs new ones. This reframing in the face of contradictions encountered in interactions with others, leads to new learning. Wittrock (1978) argues that cognitive restructuring and rehearsal are crucial to understanding and the retention of new learning.

Perkins' (1992) work has been useful in expanding thinking about the nature of understanding. He argues that deep learning involves understanding, retention and application of new learning in other contexts, rather than the 'Trivial Pursuit' theory of learning where the emphasis is on acquisition of factual information, and depth is sacrificed in favour of breadth of coverage. Perkins offers a definition of what 'understanding' of new learning might involve, taking a 'performance perspective':

> Understanding is a matter of being able to do a variety of thought-demanding things with a topic – like explaining, finding evidence and examples, generalising, applying analogising, and representing a topic in a new way.
>
> (Perkins and Blythe, 1994, p. 5)

Smith (2006) helpfully lists seven key characteristics about understanding:

- It is messy and complicated, involving the extraction of meaningful patterns from confusion.
- It is a personal process, in that we have to make our own connections in our own way.
- It is not a spectator sport. The learner has to be an active participant, making their own constructions.
- It is a social process involving communication with others and being able to explain your thinking.
- It is about performance. Learners need to have opportunities to do something with their new understanding.
- It can be difficult because it means going deeper into the learning.
- Adults can play a key role in helping young people understand, providing sensitive, well timed intervention to scaffold and mediate learning.

This has clear implications for the ways in which teachers organise the learning in the classroom to allow active engagement and demonstration of understanding in a range of different contexts.

In such a model of learning, the learners are actively involved in making meaning and making sense of new information. This requires the teacher to make links to the everyday world of children and their experiences. The teacher becomes a facilitator who is more concerned with encouraging children to explain their thinking and learning by asking the right kinds of questions, rather than a giver of knowledge. The aim of the teacher is to help the children to make connections between what they already know and what they are learning and thus to gain new insights. This means that the teacher has to have an open mind about the potential of the children in front of them and not a fixed view of each child's ability and a consequent set of matching expectations. These ideas are very close to those expressed in the Primary Memorandum (SOED, 1965) and are as relevant today as they were ahead of their time in 1965. The teacher needs to be prepared to 'go on a journey' beside the children, and allow the child some part responsibility in the process. The teacher is still the lead learner in the room and will have designed aspects of the journey very carefully, but the children must be given the opportunity to make a genuine contribution to their own learning: not only because it is essentially respectful of children, but because it makes for more effective, long-term understanding of new learning (Carnell and Lodge, 2002).

Relating the material for learning to the experience of the learner is also crucial. Learners' experiences and abilities should be the obvious starting-point for other learning. Teachers need to know about past experience to be able to build upon it and learning is less effective when the teacher does not have or value this information.

Carnell and Lodge (2002) describe co-constructivism as an expanded version of the above model, which takes a holistic view of learners and where collaboration becomes an essential dimension of the process:

> The model of co-constructivist learning . . . is not common in schools . . . it encourages the kind of learning young people need for their lives in the 21st century. It encourages confidence in dealing with complexity, flexibility and making connections. It encourages people to learn together and above all, it can help learners to become more explicit about their learning. There is a need for more of this model in schools . . . The dominant model in schools remains the reception model, reinforced through the external pressure to cover the curriculum, by teachers' historical role, their view of learners and the culture of schools.
>
> (Carnell and Lodge, 2002, p. 16)

The opportunity for children to have learning dialogues with one another has not been widely available in primary classrooms in Scotland. However, as part of the AifL initiative teachers are beginning to experiment with pair work more often as part of their teaching repertoire. This dialogue is necessary for the development of social, as well as academic, skills and requires the teacher to design learning in a different way. Collaborative working is not the normal pattern of group work in most Scottish primary schools. Whole-class teaching has become increasingly common, and often, where children are physically sitting in groups, they are actually working as a collection of individuals. The change to real collaborative working requires a huge shift of thinking on the part of teachers. It is common for teachers to reprimand children for discussing their work with their peers. However, as has been outlined in Chapter 1, there are forces currently at work in Scottish education which are beginning to change that scenario. The influence of AifL cannot be underestimated and there is evidence of shifting practice in this area.

Formative assessment

The work of Black and Wiliam (1998a, 1998b) has been significant in providing both research evidence and practical advice in relation to the most effective instructional strategies. Their wide-ranging review of the research has focused attention not only on the ways in which teachers and pupils interact with one another, but also on the interactions between pupils, in the normal day-to-day work in the classroom. It shows very clearly that effective formative assessment and effective teaching are inextricably linked. They identify five key strategies for teachers:

- engineering effective classroom discussions
- providing feedback that moves learners forward
- sharing learning intentions and success criteria with learners
- activating students as owners of their own learning
- activating students as learning resources for one another.

Teachers' planning will therefore become a key factor. Learning intentions need to be clearly identified before they can be shared. Careful design of activities and tasks is crucial and this requires the teacher to have some depth of understanding about the principles involved. The focus on the child's developing understanding is at the heart of the process, and dialogue between the teacher and learner is the vehicle by which the teacher can assess levels of understanding. The teacher's role is therefore significant – do they rely largely on factual questions, do they deliberately lead the child towards the 'right' answer, how much thinking time do they give after asking a question, do they answer the questions themselves, do they rely on the same few children to respond?

> the teacher, by lowering the level of questions and by accepting answers from a few, can keep the lesson going but is actually out of touch with the understanding of most of the class. The question/answer dialogue becomes a ritual, one in which thoughtful involvement suffers.
>
> (Black and Wiliam, 1998a, p. 11)

The skills required to handle this dialogue are considerable. The teacher needs to be able to adjust their teaching in response to the children's responses and learning needs. This skill is at the heart of effective teaching and happens in countless encounters between teacher and child during the course of the school day. Lack of responsiveness and flexibility at this point will reduce the effectiveness of the teaching.

Black and Wiliam recommend higher levels of participation through pair and group work and a stronger focus on exploring understanding rather than seeking out the 'right' answer the teacher was looking for. The development of the skill of effective questioning is therefore an essential dimension of support for teachers in changing their approaches in the classroom.

The whole area of feedback is explored in depth in the reviewed research. The development of useful, child-friendly success criteria is essential. These allow both children and teacher to assess the extent to which learning intentions have been achieved. Effective, shared success criteria allow the teacher to concentrate on the child's steps towards the learning intentions and to identify possible barriers to their understanding. Self and peer assessment can be incorporated into the learning process where learning intentions and success criteria are clearly identified and shared with children. Rather than relying on grades, teachers are encouraged to give more specific feedback, which helps children to work out what to do to improve the piece of work in question. The learner needs focused advice on strengths and areas for development in order to improve learning. To be able to provide this type of feedback, a teacher needs to be aware of the levels of understanding of the learners in their classroom and identify the best ways to increase them.

The important work done by Black and Wiliam (1998a, 1998b) has been built upon by others. Over the past five years Shirley Clarke (2001, 2003, 2005) has been writing accessible, research-informed material, giving practical advice for teachers, head teachers and local authorities in relation to formative assessment. In the introduction to her most recent book (Clarke, 2005) she refers to formative assessment as a 'living, breathing, evolving animal' (p. 2) and points to the rapid pace of development in England and Wales. The AifL initiative has meant a similar pace of development is emerging in Scotland.

Clarke gives useful overviews of the research base upon which formative assessment strategies are constructed and translates these into detailed advice for teachers. Across her three most recent publications, she has focused on planning, learning intentions, success criteria, effective feedback, questioning, self and peer evaluation, all of which are key components of effective formative assessment. She covers these in commendable practical detail for teachers, translating theory into practice in language that teachers seem to find accessible. For the purposes of this book, one of the most important areas she covers is the crucial dimension of classroom culture – the learning culture in which formative feedback can exist. She describes this as the constructivist classroom and points to the challenges for teachers in relinquishing control. She talks about motivation, self-esteem and the social context of learning, which will be explored in detail in Chapter 4, and sums up the key principles of the desired learning culture thus:

- Formative assessment depends on a constructivist classroom.
- We need to plan for different intelligences and styles of learning.
- Effort should be applauded as much as achievement.
- Many traditions of Western education lower children's self-efficacy.
- We should focus on a learning orientation rather than a performance orientation.
- The social context plays a powerful part in motivation and the effectiveness of learning.

Much of the above is important in the creation of a learning community in the classroom and the links between key features of formative assessment and key features of learning communities in the classroom are clear. Formative assessment has become a significant influence in the UK generally, and in Scotland in particular. AifL has offered practical opportunities, based on research, for the development of classrooms where learning can be organized differently. A Curriculum for Excellence provides the perfect backdrop for changing pedagogy.

Co-operative learning

Together with the major policy context of AifL and A Curriculum for Excellence, another growing development in Scottish schools is the use of co-operative learning (CL). The model has been adopted by North Lanarkshire Education Department, the second largest local authority in Scotland. They are in the process of training all their teachers in the use of co-operative learning and see clear connections with a Curriculum for Excellence and their policy on raising achievement. The particular model has emerged from successful work in co-operative learning in Durham, Canada, based mostly on the work of Johnson and Johnson (1989). Canadian trainers have worked extensively with school staff in North Lanarkshire and have supported the training of local support staff to develop the approach in classrooms throughout the local authority. They are also working with many other local authorities in Scotland who are interested in this way of working.

There have been many training programmes and a wealth of new initiatives in Scottish schools over the years, however none has been underpinned by such strong research evidence of its effectiveness. Co-operative learning has a long history as an instructional strategy with a considerable theoretical and research base. This strong theoretical and research base has been widely translated into clear instructional strategies that can be used in practice. A wide range of co-operative learning is available to teachers, ranging from very specific and prescriptive strategies to more general approaches and which require a greater conceptual understanding on the part of the teacher. Slavin (1995) describes it as having moved into the mainstream of educational practice. This is so for a number of reasons:

- There is extensive research linking CL to improved achievement and social skills

- There is a need in the twenty-first century for children to learn how to think, solve problems, integrate their knowledge and apply their skills.

- CL makes heterogeneity a resource rather than a problem.

- CL has a positive influence on social relations with minority groups in mainstream schools.

- CL fits with current conceptions of learning as social, cultural and interpersonal constructive process.

(Veenman *et al.*, 2002, p. 282)

At least three general theoretical perspectives have informed the development of co-operative learning as an instructional strategy: cognitive development, social interdependence and behavioural learning. Social interdependence theory evolved from Lewin's (1935) work on drive for goal accomplishment and intrinsic reward. Deutsch's (1949) theory about positive and negative interdependence and their effects on promotive or oppositional interaction have been a major conceptual underpinning of co-operative learning. His theory of co-operation and competition was influential on Johnson and Johnson (1989, 1999) who extended the work into social interdependence theory:

> How social interdependence is structured determines how individuals interact within the situation, which in turn, affects outcomes. More specifically, co-operation exists when positive interdependence is structured, which results in individuals interacting in ways which promote each other's success, which, in turn, generally leads to higher productivity and achievement, more positive relationships among individuals, and greater psychological health and well-being.

(Johnson and Johnson, 1989, p. 5)

Johnson and Johnson's (1993) model identifies five basic elements which should be built into activities for effective co-operation, and the practicalities of the approach will be explored in detail in Chapter 4:

- positive interdependence
- individual and group accountability
- explicit teaching of social skills
- face-to-face promotive interaction
- group processing of learning.

There is extensive research into the effectiveness of co-operative learning as a particular method of structuring this social interaction which increases pupil attainment. The Johnson *et al.* review (2000) of over 900 studies carried out on the relative benefits of co-operative, competitive and individualistic learning demonstrate the effectiveness of the methodology. The breadth of this research provides a solid basis for the conclusions drawn. They identify three major benefits to co-operative learning: higher achievement and greater productivity, more positive relationships and greater psychological health, social competence and self-esteem. They argue that there may be no other teaching strategy that simultaneously achieves so many different outcomes.

Alongside this development of co-operative learning in Scotland, is the Critical Skills Programme (CSP) promoted by Network Educational Press in Scotland, and gaining increasing numbers of practitioners (Weatherley, 2000). The training manual for CSP describes the approach as:

> a practical response from teachers working in real classrooms to the theoretical arguments supporting constructivist, collaborative, experiential, authentic and democratic learning environments. CSP can provide a real life 'how-to' model to address the worthy ideals espoused throughout recent literature.
>
> (CSP, 1997, p. 3)

CSP approaches to learning are clearly in line with a constructivist perspective and lend themselves to systematic social interaction as part of learning, with many opportunities built into the design of activities for explanation to a team member or for presentation to the class as a whole, to perform understanding. The pedagogy involved seeks to promote a set of prescribed skills: problem-solving, decision-making, critical thinking, creative thinking, communication, organisation, management and leadership; and fundamental dispositions: positive attitude to lifelong learning, self-direction, internal model of quality, collaboration, integrity and ethical character, curiosity and wonder, and community membership.

CSP has recently been deployed in every school on the island of Jersey, as well as in individual schools in many other local authorities in the UK. Wragg *et al.* (2004) undertook an evaluation of the Jersey experiment and were extremely positive about its impact on learning and teaching. In an evaluation of the approach in Glasgow, Baron *et al.* (2004) identified substantial preliminary achievements, not least that a number of staff were enthused to review their fundamental educational stance, and the exploration of the possibility of meeting national and local curriculum requirements in innovative ways. However, the issue of sustainability was more problematic. Wider coverage of a larger number of staff seemed desirable, yet difficult to achieve given the costs of training. The level of on-going staff development and support appeared to be a crucial factor in successful implementation.

Theory into practice?

Co-operative learning is a model of organising the learning environment, with a substantial theoretical and research base. The evidence of its success is, however, tempered with many warnings about the gap between the theoretical model outlined by research/developers and the practice as implemented by classroom teachers. Gillies and Ashman (2003) have reminded us that the structure is of itself important. Antil *et al.* (1998), Veenman *et al.* (2000) and Lopata *et al.* (2003) all point to discrepancies between very specific theoretical models and the practice of even experienced classroom teachers. Teachers were routinely found to adapt and modify their approach in the classroom, often omitting key elements of the model that are crucial to its overall success. This gap between theory and practice will be explored in more detail in subsequent chapters. Black and Wiliam acknowledge the problem:

> Teachers will not take up attractive sounding ideas, albeit based on extensive research, if these are presented as general principles which leave entirely to them the task of translating them into everyday practice – their classroom lives are too busy and too fragile for this to be possible for all but an outstanding few. What they need is a variety of living examples of implementation, by teachers with whom they can identify and from whom they can both derive conviction and confidence that they can do better, and see concrete examples of what doing better means in practice.
>
> (Black and Wiliam, 1998b, p. 15)

Despite the best evidence from the research, there is a certain security for teachers in ticking off the boxes 'proving' what has been *taught* or *covered*, often at the expense of focusing on what has actually been *learned*. This is hardly surprising in an environment where accountability is related to coverage of the curriculum, whether in terms of 5–14 levels or pages of the relevant language or mathematics schemes. There is an enormous pressure on teachers to cover the curriculum, and schools often respond by identifying suitable resources and/or checklists of learning outcomes from the 5–14 guidelines, and setting targets for coverage over the term or year. I have spent many hours in classrooms all over west central Scotland and the pressure felt by teachers to keep moving through the work is real. They often feel they need to move on to the 'next thing' even though they know there is no real depth of understanding. This tension between curriculum coverage and depth of understanding is at the heart of the dilemma faced by teachers in Scottish schools.

In their classrooms teachers can choose to take brave decisions to teach in ways which are more related to real learning and we will explore those alternatives in this book. The courage to go against the tide can be hard to find in the climate of tick boxes to make sure we 'cover the curriculum'. Accountability is a driving force for school managers and therefore for teachers. Those tick boxes are about helping us to feel better about what we've achieved in the classroom, feel safer when someone comes to check what we are doing. *What* we are doing seems to be more important than *why* or *how*. We then descend into the mechanistic checklist mentality which many teachers find so mind-numbing, time-consuming and unhelpful for learning. The quality of actual learning has not always been the focus assessment. Dewey described coverage is the enemy of comprehension (Dewey, 1963)

A Curriculum for Excellence has provided a chink of light at the end of that tunnel: a framework for learning which, unlike the 5–14 curriculum, encourages emphasis on depth, as well as breadth. AifL has offered teachers the opportunity to examine their practice and consider viable, attractive, alternatives which are much more clearly focused on the quality of the child's learning rather than the quantity of curriculum content. Of course, time will tell, and the restrictions teachers feel will not be lifted overnight, but there is a significant change in the policy context that may, in time, facilitate an equally significant change in practice in the classroom. Along-side these policy contexts, the gradual introduction of co-operative learning strategies into many Scottish schools presents a picture of real possibility for change in the practices of large numbers of primary school teachers and the creation of conditions conducive to the building of learning communities in their classrooms.

So it is important for teachers to hang on to what they know to be central. Most teachers know good teaching when they experience it and can identify effective learning when it is happening in their classrooms. That is why forays into formative assessment and co-operative learning strategies have been so successful. However, we must never underestimate the courage required to go against the grain, to try something new or different, to challenge the status quo.

The changes required to move to this model of teaching are significant for many teachers as they rely less on the expertise of the teacher in explaining and transmitting new learning, and more on active participation of learners in genuinely shared dialogues. These will be explored more fully in Chapter 3.

Chapter 3

PROFESSIONAL SELF-KNOWLEDGE

The ideas discussed in the next two chapters are very closely linked. I argue that the whole area of building community and effective learning relationships in the classroom cannot really be separated from the identity of the teacher. Learning and teaching do not take place within a vacuum. The historical, social and political context already discussed has a major influence on teachers' perceptions of themselves and their profession. The wider context of education affects teachers daily in their classrooms and much of it is outwith their immediate control. The feeling of lack of control over a rapidly changing educational landscape contributes, for many teachers, to feelings of frustration and disillusionment. Many came into the job with high, but different expectations and find it hard to maintain their enthusiasm and confidence in the face of increasing public accountability and decreasing public confidence. Schools are often held responsible for, or seen as the solution to, any number of social and political problems, so it is not surprising that teachers' confidence and surefootedness are knocked. This can show itself in a number of possible ways, from stress-related absence to deep cynicism about all aspects of the job. Although it is important for teachers to become aware of the social and political context of education, their responses to change, pressure and the context in which they find themselves working are a very personal and individual matter.

Covey (1992) has written about this space between stimulus and response and argues that in order to deal effectively with the external circumstances of our lives, we need to develop our inner selves. He uses the term 'inside-out' as a strategy for doing this. ' "Inside-out" means to start first with self; even more fundamentally, to start with the most *inside* part of self – with your paradigms, your character, and your motives' (pp. 42–3).

The capacity to connect effectively with others is directly related to our capacity to understand our own motivation and to feel comfortable in our own skins. Covey advocates proactivity, and describes the space between stimulus and response as the place where individuals can *choose* how they react to any given situation. This is not to deny the very real external influences on people, but emphasises the possibility of taking some control over your reactions to the situations in which you find yourself. He suggests that our confidence and effectiveness will grow in direct proportion to the amount of control we can manage to take of some aspects of our lives. He explains this in terms of working within your circle of influence and circle of concern, and argues that the more time you spend in your circle of influence, the bigger it will become. So, in practical terms this means that in being proactive about our lives, we need to spend less time being concerned or worrying about those aspects about which we can do nothing, and spend more of our energies on those aspects where we can make a difference. This is not to discount the possibility of collective action on bigger issues, but rather to focus energy on where it will make most difference. It would therefore be important for teachers to make themselves aware of the external forces at work in education, in order to be able to explore where they may or may not have any real influence as an individual.

Figure 3.1 (adapted from Covey, 1992, p. 82)

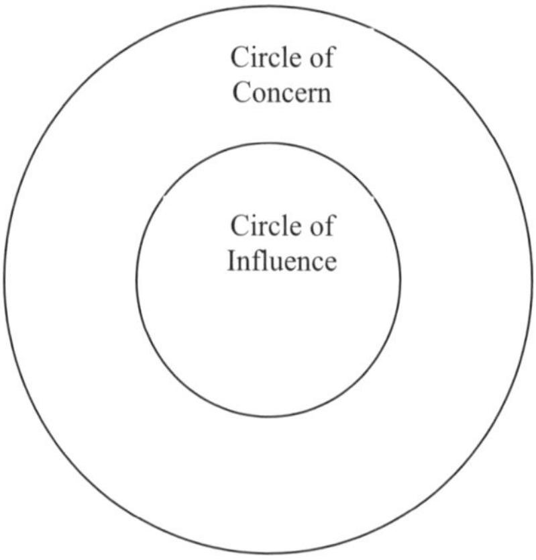

Such an approach can be very empowering and liberating. It offers the possibility that we need not be victims of circumstance, but can be proactive. In the longer term, we also reduce the stress of worrying about things we can do nothing about and increase our sense of having some measure of control over our lives. Clearly there are big social, political and economic issues that affect us in fundamental ways, and of course teachers will involve themselves in these, but this way of looking at the world opens up possibilities for working more effectively within those parameters in our own daily lives. And for teachers, this means that, as individuals, they can make choices about how they react to their changing professional world. They can work within their own circle of influence in the classroom and make a difference in the areas where they have control over how things are done.

Teachers have an enormous area of influence; what happens every day in the classroom is very much within their control and the choices they make here have a significant effect on the children they teach. The mindset of the teacher is a decisive factor in the creation of the atmosphere of the class.

So there is a very individual and personal dimension to effective teaching, which must also be considered, alongside the wider context of education. Covey's work (1992) is helpful in exploring the extent to which our inner sense of self affects our ability to then relate to others effectively. He urges us to explore that inner world by defining for ourselves the values and principles that underpin the lens through which we view the world. This is important work which helps us clarify our sense of purpose and gives us a compass with which to navigate the terrain of daily life. These basic paradigms inform our attitudes and behaviours:

> What teachers do, how they teach, is shaped primarily by what they believe about learning and learners, rather than by what they are told to do by any textbook or course description.
>
> (SCCC, 1996, p. iii)

Palmer's (1998) work also explores this inner world, but specifically in relation to teachers and teaching. He argues that good teaching is based on self-knowledge and advocates exploring 'the inner landscape of the teaching self' (p. 2). This is important for the development of a sense of professional identity; an understanding of their own personal stance and how that relates to values and beliefs. He believes that good teaching cannot be reduced to technique alone, but comes from the identity and integrity of the teacher, so that the 'Who?' of teaching is more important than the 'What?' 'How?' or even the 'Why?' The more familiar teachers are with their inner terrain, the more surefooted their teaching will be.

These are powerful ideas that are not explored often enough in the discourse about changing pedagogy in teacher education arenas and in schools. We mostly concentrate on the ways in which teachers can be supported to implement new methodologies in practical terms: the structures in place in schools, the staff development opportunities and resources available, and coaching in context. We tend not to spend time discussing how these new methodologies fit with a teacher's beliefs about learning and learners. Indeed we rarely give teachers the space to examine those beliefs, even though they are central to their daily work. Brookfield (1995) urges teachers to do just that by reflecting on practice: to 'hunt the assumptions' in their teaching and begin to identify their own deeply held beliefs.

This chapter examines these key areas of influence on the levels of teachers' professional self-knowledge, and the impact of that self-knowledge on the creation of communities of learning in their classrooms.

The inner world of the teacher: working from the inside out

The premise is that before teachers are in a position to feel comfortable building learning communities in their classrooms, they need to feel comfortable with their own identity as a teacher. They need a sense of inner confidence about their teaching, about their views on learning and their ability to relate effectively to children. No matter how much curricular and technical knowledge a teacher may have, there are other important skills and understandings needed to build productive relationships with children, which are arguably more difficult to acquire, and less likely to have been developed in initial teacher education traditionally. These affective areas of teaching are the ones which often trouble teachers the most. Most teachers can easily gain and update curricular knowledge or technical strategies, but the quality of the relationships they do or don't form with the children in their class affect them personally, and serious challenges arise if those classroom relationships are not mutually respectful. Yet opportunities to focus on the development of the affective area of teaching are few and far between. Central to the argument then is the notion that the development of personal intelligence is vital to effective relationships. Gardner (1983) identified personal intelligence within his theory of multiple intelligences.

*Inter*personal intelligence 'denotes a person's capacity to understand the intentions, motivations and desires of other people and, consequently to work effectively with others' (Gardner, 1999, p. 43). He suggests teachers as being amongst those specified groups for whom acute interpersonal intelligence is crucial. This intelligence includes the potential to read the moods of others, including the appraisal of non-verbal messages, and the ability to empathise with another's feelings. *Intra*personal intelligence 'involves the capacity to understand oneself, to have an effective working model of oneself – including one's own desires, fears, and capacities' (Gardner, 1999 p. 43). This kind of self-knowledge and self-awareness is closely connected to the capacity to then relate to others – important skills indeed for an effective teacher.

The concept of emotional intelligence, first proposed by Salovey and Mayer (1990) and popularised and broadened further by Goleman (1995). stems in part from Gardner's work. Goleman differentiates between intellectual and emotional intelligence and makes a similar distinction between personal and social competence. He adapted Mayer's model and identified five basic social and emotional competencies: self-awareness, self-regulation, motivation, empathy and social skills. The two dimensions of emotional intelligence, personal and social, are related, and this awareness of one's own and others' feelings, needs and concerns, as well as skill at handling them, seem to be particularly relevant for teachers in connecting with learners.

As Day argues, teaching involves emotional labour:

> Teachers invest their personal and professional selves in their work-place. Thus, because their work is a principal location for teachers' sense of self-esteem and personal as well as professional satisfaction, it is inevitable that they will have deeply felt emotions. Maintaining an awareness of the tensions in managing our emotions is part of the safeguard and joy of teaching.
>
> (Day, 2004, p. 45)

Covey (1998) stresses the importance of working from the 'inside-out' in this way, establishing an inner confidence and self-awareness before working on the skills required to deal more effectively with others. The link between the two is the link between this chapter and the next. I argue that the inner terrain of the teacher is a crucial starting-point for the building of effective learning communities, whether in the classroom with learners, or outside the classroom with professional colleagues. The teacher needs to have inner strength and confidence to be able to engage with children and learning in the quite demanding ways outlined in this book. Traditional approaches to teaching and learning allow the teacher to remain at a greater distance from the learners and to retain considerable control of all that goes on in the classroom:

> Teaching is a daily exercise in vulnerability . . . Unlike many professions, teaching is always done at the dangerous intersection of personal and public life . . . As we try to connect ourselves and our subjects with our students, we make ourselves, as well as our subjects, vulnerable to indifference, judgement, ridicule. To reduce our vulnerability, we disconnect from students, from subjects, and even from ourselves. We build a wall between inner truth and outer performance, and we play-act the teacher's part.
>
> (Palmer, 1998, p. 17)

It is not a simple matter of choosing to adopt a new strategy one day, and putting it into practice the next. It is a complex mixture of personal and professional challenges which run deep into the beliefs and values the teacher brings to the classroom. The balance of power needs to shift and that requires a fundamental renegotiation of intellectual authority in the class-room, which challenges deep-seated assumptions about the roles of teachers and learners. The ability to recognise and negotiate that shift is at the heart of the success or otherwise of implementing the kinds of changes advocated in this book and professional self-knowledge is a key dimension.

The good news is that emotional intelligence is not fixed and can be developed in the light of experience and understanding (Goleman, 1996). People can increase their own self- awareness through critical reflection, by examining the values which underpin their perceptions and actions. They can learn to interact differently with others and improve the effectiveness of their communication (Covey, 1998; Gillen, 1992). Appropriate personal development opportunities are helpful in the process and we will explore those in more detail in Chapter 5.

The importance of critical reflection

Critical reflection is a key dimension of the development of professional self- knowledge. Whether done alone, in writing, or together with others in a supportive group, the process of reflecting critically on practice in the classroom can be helpful to teachers as they incorporate new ways of working in the classroom. As the teacher moves from one way of organising learning where they felt quite comfortable, to a new one where they feel less secure, they are likely to experience crises of confidence. It is helpful to take the space and time to step back from the teaching and, if possible, to share the concerns and successes of real-life teaching with others who understand the context. The process of critical reflection is in itself worthwhile, offering teachers the opportunity to clarify their own thoughts and feelings and then share them with others in similar contexts. This process is more than simply reflecting on the practicalities of lessons: it involves a deeper level of exam-ination of personal perspectives and a wider context than the classroom.

Brookfield (1995) argues that critical reflection is important for a number of reasons. He points to the benefits of the process, but places it within the bigger picture of the power relationships of the political, social and economic context. It is possible for teachers to use reflective practice to unearth assumptions about the wider ideological context of their work, that allow them to identify the possibilities of their influence as individuals. For the purposes of this chapter, it is particularly relevant to focus on the fact that critical reflection helps teachers develop a rationale for practice, an informed commitment to core beliefs and values, and a foundational refer-ence point for their work. He suggests we should look at what we do from as many different angles as possible and offers four possible lenses to illu-minate our teaching and our assumptions:

- Our autobiographies as learners and teachers are an important source of understanding of our own practice. Our own experi-ences of learning are felt at an emotional level. These are deep experiences and long-lasting influences, which affect us power-fully, and make a good starting-point to help us explain those parts of our practice to which we feel strongly committed.

- Our students' feedback helps us teach more responsively.

- Our colleagues' shared experiences allow us to engage in critical conversations to check our reading of a problem, reactions, assumptions and justifications against others. Ultimately critical reflection is a collaborative venture.

● Theoretical literature also offers an alternative interpretive framework through which we can try to make sense of our practice.

These are very useful tools to encourage teachers to explore critically their own beliefs, as well as the practices that flow from those beliefs. Using all these lenses to reflect critically on our practice helps us to get a range of perspectives on our teaching, and a more informed view of how we go about our business.

Autobiographical reflection

This is a crucial dimension in exploring our deeply rooted assumptions about teaching and learning:

> We may espouse philosophies of teaching that we have learned from formal study, but the most significant and most deeply embedded influences that operate on us are the images, models, and conceptions of teaching derived from our experiences as learners.
>
> (Brookfield, 1995, p. 49)

For this reason it is crucial that teachers be given the opportunity to spend time reflecting on these experiences of learning and the impact they may have had on their views about teaching. There are clearly dangers of self-deception in such introspective, subjective examination of autobiographical detail. Having a keen awareness of the limitations of the process, and working in structured ways, often with colleagues, to gain other perspectives can balance the process. However a key feature of autobiographical reflection is the understanding gained from being in the position of learner. The insights gained about what makes learning easy or difficult are gained from experiencing the power dynamic of the teacher–learner relationship especially as an adult, and there are few substitutes for the real thing. When placed in this context, as a learner, the elements of effective, successful learning become clear, and provide valuable information for future teaching.

Children's feedback

Children's feedback on their experience of learning is another important dimension of interrogating teachers' assumptions about learning and teaching in the classroom. Brookfield (1995) emphasises the importance of what he describes as getting inside the students' heads and finding out what they are thinking. Of course, this depends on teachers' willingness to open up the discussion about effective learning with the children, and that in itself requires a certain amount of confidence, especially if they are likely to uncover personal criticism in the process. But if it can become part of the teacher's routine evaluation process, it can provide vital evidence to inform subsequent practice. It is an important source of information to help teachers get in touch with the reality of the learning in their classroom, as opposed to their own mental model of what they think takes place. This is very challenging, since we often hear things we don't recognise or want to hear, but if we want to hunt our assumptions, we need this feedback.

> The most powerful way you can communicate what you stand for as a teacher is to make sure that you practise what you teach . . . And the only way you'll know how well you're modelling these values and processes is by seeing your actions through students' eyes.
>
> (Brookfield, 1995, pp. 112–13)

The impact on the learners of being given respect, equality, and having their views taken seriously is significant and will be explored in Chapter 4.

Reflection becomes critical when it examines the power relationships which affect learning, and when it questions our assumptions and practices. The power relationships in the classroom are a central area of concern in this book and are the focus of much of the reflection teachers are encouraged to do. Critical reflection of the type described above increases democratic trust in the classroom. When we make honest efforts to find out how children are experiencing our teaching, we model the self-evaluation that we are encouraging in our learners. This process of enabling effective feedback also presents difficulties in gathering honest, authentic opinion from children, especially given the power relationships in the classroom. It is, however, worthy of serious consideration and will be explored in Chapter 5, where it is particularly relevant to the establishment of a learning community in the classroom. Strategies to tackle this area with children will also be examined.

Sharing our experience with colleagues

This is essentially about creating communities of learning for teachers. The creation of such communities of learning is possibly just as important for teachers as for learners. Kohn (1996) emphasises the importance of the culture created in schools where teachers are themselves members of learning communities; such a culture increases the likelihood of those teachers recreating such a sense of community in their own classrooms. Brookfield (1995, p. 141) describes critical reflection as ' an irreducibly social process' and points to the benefits of sharing practice to gain new insights but also to realise the commonality of experience. Palmer recognises the importance of the collegiate support for professionals who are in the process of changing their approaches to teaching and learning. The risks involved in changing practice are significant and teachers can benefit enormously from the long-term support of colleagues who are experiencing the same doubts:

> The growth of any craft depends on shared practice and honest dialogue among people who do it. We grow by private trial and error, to be sure – but our willingness to try, and fail, as individuals is severely limited when we are not supported by a community that encourages such risks . . . Good talk about good teaching is what we need – to enhance both our professional practice and the selfhood that comes from it.
>
> (Palmer, 1998, p. 144)

He advocates the sharing of critical moments in teaching and learning in an open and honest way, where teachers identify their struggles and successes and get the opportunity to discuss their teaching methods. It is not always easy for teachers to openly discuss their fears and struggles in the classroom and the culture of the school is vital in providing the kind of atmosphere where teachers feel comfortable discussing these difficult issues. Teachers need to feel assured that the benefits will outweigh the risks.

The successful example of learning communities used to develop teachers' expertise in formative assessment practices suggests the model could be effective for the following reasons:

- It emphasises the teacher-as-local-expert.
- It offers the possibility of sustaining a school-embedded model over time.
- The non-threatening context allows teachers to identify their own areas for development and get help with these in discussion with their colleagues.
- The real-life stories of colleagues' experiences give the support teachers need to take risks.
- It provides a forum for supporting teachers in converting the broad strategies into 'lived' practices within their classrooms.

(Wiliam and Thompson, 2006, p. 15)

Time for study, consultation and reflection is identified by Eraut (1994) as an important dimension of support for professional learning. McLaughlin and Marsh (1978) conclude that training sessions will have only short-term effects if not backed up by longer term on-site support for staff as they begin to internalise the ideas learned and that teacher learning is a long-term process involving experimentation, reflection and problem-solving. Teachers need time to develop their own interpretations and make sense of the new learning. Teacher learning communities where colleagues can reflect together, afford teachers the opportunity to do this.

Even experienced teachers do not find adopting new ideas and practices an easy task. It could be described as a leap of faith. It is scary. Brookfield (1995) describes it as leaving solid ground, when even for the most eager practitioner, enthusiasm can turn to terror – like the cartoon figure who runs off the cliff and finds himself pedalling in mid air above the canyon. Brookfield urges us to be prepared and take a parachute. That 'parachute' can be a peer learning community, where private anxieties can be commonly experienced and demystified.

Theoretical literature

The literature is, of course, helpful to teachers as a lens through which to view their teaching, to try to make sense of their beliefs and practices against theoretical frameworks, and to examine alternatives. Brookfield (1995) believes that reading theory assists critical reflection in five main ways:

- Theory lets us 'name' our practice.
- It helps break the circle of familiarity.
- Theory can be a substitute for absent colleagues.
- It prevents group think and improves conversation with colleagues.
- Theory locates our practice in a social context.

Engaging with theory is not a task teachers always find attractive. Much of the theoretical literature on critical reflection is quite impenetrable and only adds to some teachers' sense of inadequacy. They often say they have little time for such reading and reflection in their busy professional lives, but if they do want to be considered professional, they have to think about what that means in terms of being aware of the literature in their field and the implications for practice. We need to find ways of making these theoretical frameworks more accessible to busy professionals, especially as their reluctance to engage in theoretical discussions of their area of expertise is used by policy-makers and public alike to reduce them to technicians rather than professionals. Smith (2001, 2005, 2006) has made many worthy efforts to encapsulate key ideas from extensive reading and present them to teachers in a user-friendly format. Perhaps when they have dipped into the ideas in this way they will be motivated to read more widely. This is a good starting-point for many teachers, although we should remain alert to the possibility of the dumbing down of teachers, if they are viewed as professionals who do not engage in theoretical debate.

However, as with each of the above lenses through which Brookfield encourages us to examine our assumptions, the paradox is clear: teachers need to first be willing to engage in the process of critical reflection. Thereafter, becoming critically reflective takes hard work. It is challenging at many levels, not least because it leads to uncertainty. It is best shared or it may exacerbate lack of confidence. Brookfield (1995) encourages teachers to let go of their quest for certainties and neat solutions in their work, and to share their doubts and concerns with others who understand the context. In doing this they will help to demystify the complex process of teaching and the sense that many teachers have, isolated in their classroom, that they are somehow not doing the job just as well as everyone else in the school.

Fullan identifies at least three important issues to be addressed in implementing change in practice:

- the possible use of new materials
- the possible use of new teaching approaches
- the possible alteration of beliefs.

(Fullan, 1995, p. 39)

The first two are easier to achieve than the last, and yet the shift in beliefs is crucial for real change to take place. Fullan points out the extra difficulty in relation to working at this level of the often unstated and unexamined nature of these beliefs, which supports earlier arguments for critical reflection as an essential component of pedagogical change. A conceptual understanding of the new approaches to teaching is required if fundamental change is to take place. This level of understanding allows the teacher to make informed choices about planning and implementation and to be in a position to justify the change to herself and to others. 'In other words, changes in beliefs and understanding (first principles) are the foundation of achieving lasting reform' (p. 45).

However, Fullan also suggests that addressing beliefs may be more usefully done after teachers have experienced some initial attempts at the new approaches in their classrooms. He also emphasises the long -term nature of this development work and the relevance of professional learning communities in this context. Essentially the depth of change and shift in understanding relates not just to what teachers do, but what they think. This means that training cannot be about practical application of technique alone, but must address these more complex issues of the mindset of the teacher. When the teacher is fully engaged at all these three levels there is much stronger chance of increased confidence and motivation to implement new approaches. The development of meaning is at the heart of the change process and that has to be done by individuals, often in many different ways.

We can argue about whether a change of beliefs precedes or follows a change in resources or knowledge, or practices, but there can be no doubt that beliefs have to eventually shift in order for real and lasting change to take place. The approaches to learning and teaching being promoted in this book require teachers to address these difficult issues.

It is important that there is coherence between the teaching methods being used and the teacher's beliefs about learning and learners. Where there is dissonance, teachers will revert to tried and tested strategies with which they feel comfortable. The challenge is that creating a learning community in the classroom calls for much more than just a change of instructional strategies, although this is a crucial element. It requires the teacher to be comfortable with a changed relationship with learners and a fundamental shift in the power relationships in the classroom.

Professional self-knowledge – creating a community of learning

Teachers are unlikely to invest the considerable energy required to change over to this way of working if they are fundamentally opposed to the philosophy which underpins it:

- If they feel uncomfortable handing over some of the power in the classroom to children, they will struggle to commit to this way of organising learning.

- If they believe that children are not able to take responsibility for their own learning, they are unlikely to give them opportunities to learn those skills.

- If they think that the teacher needs to do most of the talking and the teaching, they are unlikely to organise the learning to allow children the opportunity to engage with one another to share and clarify their thinking.

- If they believe that their children don't have the skills to work effectively in groups, they are unlikely to design effective co-operative learning opportunities.

- If they think it is important that children are busy writing and filling in worksheets and workbooks, they are unlikely to allow them the space to become actively involved in their learning, making meaning from discussing ideas with others and relating them to their own experience.

- If they believe that children's behaviour needs to be policed with rewards and punishments, they will not be inclined to take a longer term view of encouraging children to learn to take responsibility for managing their own behaviour, rather than pleasing the teacher.

- If they believe that teacher knows best they are unlikely to engage in strategies aimed at giving children the mechanism to make comment on their experience of learning.

- If they are unaware of the delicate balance of power in operation in the classroom, they may ride rough-shod over the sensitivities of that relationship and compromise children's learning in the process, giving them no voice or say in the matters which affect their learning.

Palmer sums it up nicely:

> Community, or connectedness, is the principle behind good teaching
> . . . Like teaching itself, creating educational community can never
> be reduced to technique . . . it depends on the integrity and identity
> of the teacher.
>
> (Palmer, 1998, pp. 115–16)

I am arguing that teachers' beliefs and values are crucial in the creation of learning communities, that their unexamined assumptions impinge on the choices they make in the classroom about methodology and ethos, and that much deeper work needs to be done with teachers to explore these defining dimensions of teaching through critical reflection and personal development.

Chapter 4

CREATING A COMMUNITY OF LEARNERS

This chapter is concerned with creating and maintaining effective relationships in the classroom. Most teachers will acknowledge, at an intellectual level, the importance of effective relationships for effective learning, and much has been done in recent years to explore the ways in which teachers might promote positive behaviour and motivate children to engage with learning. However, translating those ideas into practice can sometimes be a challenge. Often the emphasis is on imposing control and order in the classroom rather than a genuine concern to create a community of learning. The gradual introduction of some of the ideas associated with Circle Time (Mosley, 1998) into most Scottish primary schools has also contributed to the notion that the emotional dimension of learning is worthy of practical attention. The idea of creating a caring learning community in the classroom is taking this notion to another level of formally structuring the routines and practices of the class to ensure all are treated with respect and given the opportunity to make a contribution to their community. Increased levels of personal and collective responsibility are encouraged, alongside a sense of belonging and emotional security. The emphasis is on co-operation, rather than competition, in an essentially democratic learning environment. The role of the teacher is crucial.

Teachers have both the right and the responsibility to develop a climate in the classroom which supports effective learning. This involves maintaining order without undermining learners' self esteem. (SCCC, 1996, p.19)

Baloche (1998) identifies three main stages in the development of community in the classroom: inclusion, shared control and influence, and appreciation and caring. She argues that groups move through these phases as different issues become more important to them. Firstly, children need to know how they fit in, that they are going to be accepted and that can feel safe and secure in the new environment. Once they feel some sense of belonging, they begin to become concerned about the level of involvement they have in the decision-making process and to what extent their voices will be heard. Eventually they want to know that they are liked and cared for in the group. This doesn't seem to be a surprising set of needs for human beings; I'm sure many of us can relate to them, yet consideration of the philosophy behind this sense of community is not often discussed explicitly as a part of classroom management strategies. Sergiovanni draws our attention to the importance of community:

> The need for community is universal. A sense of belonging, of continuity, of being connected to others and to ideas and values that make out lives meaningful and significant – these needs are shared by all of us.
>
> (Sergiovanni, 1994, p. xiii)

It is one thing to learn the techniques and strategies associated with this approach; it is quite another thing to buy into the philosophy. The extent to which teachers feel this is a necessary dimension of learning is closely related to their own professional beliefs and values: 'Good teachers possess a capacity for connectedness . . . The connections made by good teachers are not held in their methods but in their hearts' (Palmer, 1998, p. 11). This chapter is really about what is possible when teachers have the courage to teach from the heart and build authentic relationships with and among children, that are highly conducive to learning. Part of that relationship is the acknowledgement of the value of the learner's right to make a contribution to the process and to be actively involved in it. What would a learning community look like and how would we go about creating it in the classroom? What would it be like to experience it, as a learner and as a teacher? How effective would it be? I move on to address these questions now.

Individual teachers can begin the process of creating community in their own classroom. Obviously it is helpful if there is a joint or whole-school approach to the process, but large numbers of teachers will not find themselves in such fortunate circumstances, and cannot depend upon that level of support. It is necessary therefore to explore the ways in which an individual teacher can make changes in their own class that will have real impact on building community. As we have discussed in previous chapters, the teacher's motivation here is key and where the teacher is committed to changing the atmosphere of the class, it is quite possible for one class to operate in this way. Teachers, however, needs to have more than the belief in the approach; they need to have an understanding of the theoretical basis for the methodology, a range of skills to allow them to put the theory into practice and a toolbox of strategies which they can build into their teaching repertoire. The theory and the policy frameworks have been explored in earlier chapters, as has the importance of the beliefs and values that teachers bring to the classroom.

I now explore the ways in which teachers can begin to put the ideas into practice. While it may be possible for teachers to work in this kind of way without formal training and support, they are much more likely to be successful if they have a structured methodology to support their philosophy and help them translate it into practice. This book does not pretend to be a training guide; far from it. It is intended to map out the terrain and allow those interested in this way of organising learning and teaching to find out what might be involved. It aims to provide teachers with the grounding and encouragement to get started on the road to creating their own community of learners.

Information and advice on the techniques involved in the approaches outlined in this chapter can be found in a very wide range of literature and training material and it can be difficult for the interested teacher to know where to start, so I have included references for the material I have found most useful in putting these ideas into practice (see Appendix). I have been particularly influenced by the co-operative learning philosophy of Johnson and Johnson (1989, 1991, 1993, 1999), the practical advice of Baloche (1998), the ideas of Kohn (1992, 1996, 1999) on the benefits of community, the work of Palmer (1998) on teachers' beliefs and values, and the concept of critical reflection as put forward by Brookfield (1995). I have been inspired by the training of North Lanarkshire Council Education Department's Co-operative Learning and Network Educational Press' Critical Skills Programme (CSP) as catalysts for translating these ideas into practice in teacher education. These provided my grounding and encouragement. The version of co-operative learning shared below is an amalgam of the reading, reflection, training and practice I have used successfully to date.

Building community

The challenge in building effective relationships within a learning community is carving out the time to make it happen. The pressures on teachers to get through the curriculum have been mentioned several times in previous chapters and that pressure makes it increasing difficult for teachers to justify spending time on this apparently content-free learning activity. Of course the process itself is important. So teachers need to be able to justify the process to themselves and others. The process involves using and valuing children's experience, creating safe, respectful learning groups in home teams and in the class as a whole, organising effective co-operative learning, encouraging self and peer evaluation and allowing children the opportunity to give feedback on their experience of learning.

Children's experience

The use of children's experience is a key dimension in building a learning community. We ignore the 'real' lives of our learners at our peril. That is what they are most interested in, that is where their motivation usually comes from, and that should be the starting-point for their learning. School is not at the centre of the universe for all children; they do have other lives just as teachers do. Both are often ignored to the detriment of the self-esteem and motivation of those involved. It is very strange that we somehow manage to ignore this crucial dimension of our learners and often just get straight on with the work on a morning, regardless of the events of the previous day. This is not to say that we must spend hours listening to all of the endless stories children will line up to tell us each day; but it does mean we should consider structuring the day to allow opportunities for such sharing of experience. There is no point in pretending they will not talk about their experience, so we should factor it in and use it positively. Allowing children the opportunity to 'check in' by sharing their thoughts and feelings before they begin the day's work is a good way of easing them from the outside world into the classroom atmosphere and to set them up for the learning ahead. It also helps to build a sense of belonging to the class and the group which adds to the positive climate in the classroom. There are many strategies which can be used to facilitate this kind of sharing.

There are also many benefits for the teacher in this process of sharing experience. The case for getting to know the learner was being made by Dewey (1963) more than sixty years ago, yet we are still debating whether we can afford the time for this. His basic premise is acknowledged in much more recent guidance which states, 'Knowing what kind of people your learners are, and having some understanding of what they are thinking is essential for effective teaching' (SCCC, 1996, p. 17).

Approaches addressed in the co-operative learning training and the literature also allow the teacher many more opportunities to get to know something about the children in their class. This is crucial knowledge which lays the foundations for building effective relationships with each child and assisting teachers in identifying learning needs. Teachers can quickly access an enormous amount of information about what makes each child 'tick'. They build up this picture over a period of time and it allows them to make insightful choices about how to engage with individuals and what might motivate them.

The importance of using the children's own experience as a starting-point for learning has been highlighted in previous chapters, so it is crucial to build that into the planning of teaching and learning. The first place we should begin when introducing new ideas is the existing knowledge and understanding of our learners. That means organising the learning to start from the children's experience rather than the often irrelevant scenarios laid out for them in the many workbooks and textbooks in regular use in the classroom. For example, why would we teach about the 24-hour clock using the scenarios in the textbook, rather than ask children to explore its use in *their* everyday environment first of all? Children need to be helped to make connections between what they already know and what we are hoping they will learn; their own experience is the bridge between the two.

I argue children's experience needs to be at the heart of learning for three reasons: it is important to them, sharing it encourages a sense of community and belonging, and it is the most effective starting-point for making connections to new learning.

Base teams

Building community needs attention at both group and class level. It is important to allow children the time to get to know and trust one another and build a sense of strong, positive group identity, so stable learning groups should be formed. These base groups provide long-term support, encouragement and assistance. The benefits of heterogeneous teams (mixed in ability, race and sex) are well documented in this model of learning, so diversity within the group is seen as an advantage rather than a disadvantage (Johnson et al., 2000).

This is a way of creating smaller communities in the classroom, where children can build closer relationships and some kind of team spirit. The purpose of creating these base groups or home teams is to provide a reference point and a support mechanism for the children in the group. The teacher can form the groups on the basis of friendship, academic skills or social skills and they stay in these groups long enough to begin to work as a team. In order to establish some kind of group identity, the children in each group should be asked to spend some time, at the beginning, finding out about each other's interests, strengths and skills. They are encouraged to take part in team-building activities throughout the course of the year which cement the bonds in the home teams. They learn about the different strengths each team member brings to the tasks they are set. This has the added benefit of giving children the chance to see the diverse range of skills their group members might have, and balances the tendency to judge one another on the basis of membership of a particular maths or reading group.

> Again and again I have seen greater long run efficiency, learning and liking of school in classrooms if teachers take time for teambuilding and class building. When there is a positive identity, liking, respect and trust among team members and class mates, there is a context which maximum learning can occur.
>
> (Kagan, 1990, p. 269)

This group would also be the basis for a number of activities related to building community. Children would be asked to devise ground rules for working with each other, usually after a few attempts at collaborative group work, when they have experience some of the associated difficulties.

Assistance can be given by the teacher to devise these ground rules, but they should come from the children themselves and relate to the issues that face them in trying to work together effectively. These ground rules should be displayed and referred to regularly. They should be a work in progress, which the class comes back to on a regular basis to adapt and change in the light of their increasing experience of group working. The idea is to focus their attention on the process of working together and the social skills required to make it effective, as well as the product of their group work. Group members are encouraged to take part regularly in short contact activities to keep the group identity strong throughout the year.

Class community

As well as the development of a sense of community through the establishment of base groups or home teams, there is much that can be done with the class as a whole. It is important that the class identity is also nurtured. The daily rituals and routines of the class are important and this kind of community building needs to be sustained and run alongside the maintenance of groups. These intentional opportunities for children to become a cohesive group who think of themselves as 'we', have to be integrated into teachers' planning. A wide range of team or class builders can be organised to develop a sense of team, of belonging, of community. There are many strategies for this kind of work, including the use of songs, stories, sharing experiences, class meetings and regular 'games' to keep the group bonded. There are many examples of activities which serve this important function in Craigen and Ward (2004).

Many teachers use Circle Time (Mosley 1998) as a mechanism to give children the opportunity to do this. It is a democratic approach which allows children to share their thoughts and feelings with the rest of the class and to bring up issues that seem to be affecting the class community. It promotes better relationships and positive behaviour. There is also the opportunity to seek out time to talk to the teacher individually. Typically teachers introduce Circle Time as part of Personal and Social Development. It usually involves regular class meetings where the children work on a range of activities, sitting in a circle, and following clearly laid down ground rules. These Golden Rules are an important dimension of the process and are used in conjunction with Golden Time, which is an incentive system involving a weekly celebration to encourage children to keep to the rules.

There are a number of different structures which can be used in Circle Time to vary the experience: games, rounds, pairs, brainstorming, nominations for success, drama techniques, questions, discussion, reflection and calming rituals (Mosley 1998). The positive effects of Circle Time are particularly relevant to the creation of a community of learning in the classroom.

There is a strong democratic element, even to the physical arrangement of the seating, where all participants have the right to speak as well as the right to pass. Their sense of belonging, safety and trust is directly affected by activities designed to enhance self esteem and encourage open and honest communication with classmates. The teacher's role is as facilitator and the usual control is replaced by a more informal, mutually respectful atmosphere in the group.

The extent to which teachers are willing to allocate time to the kinds of activities outlined above is closely connected to the value they assign to them and their ability to then justify the use of that time. The effect of children working closely together in a structured way to build their identity as a group, in base groups or as a whole class groups, is to contribute to a community of learners who feel safe and comfortable in their learning environment, who have support mechanisms which do not always depend on the teacher, and who have a sense of responsibility towards their peers.

Working co-operatively

The building of group identity is only useful if the group is then given the opportunity to work collaboratively and put their team work to use. It is therefore essential that the teacher uses instructional strategies that require children to work co-operatively. Although it is becoming more popular, it is still not the most common methodology you will encounter in Scottish primary schools. I argue that it should be the core of teachers' repertoire since it delivers the many positive results outlined in Chapter 2.

Johnson and Johnson (1993) propose five basic elements essential for effective co-operation that provide an excellent starting-point for teachers:

- face-to-face interaction
- positive interdependence
- individual accountability
- group processing
- social skills.

Taken together, these elements combine to create a framework that delivers co-operative learning. The research base for this particular approach is impressive and it is fairly straightforward to translate it into classroom practice.

Face-to-face interaction

The physical arrangement of the group is vitally important. Group work is organised so that members of the group *have* to interact with one another to complete the task, so high levels of participation are crucial. Children should therefore sit face to face and be close enough that they can share materials, maintain eye contact with all group members, talk to each other quietly and exchange ideas in a comfortable atmosphere. The difference it makes to have children sit this way is significant and it is worth rearranging furniture. Four is the ideal size of group because it allows several different pairings (shoulder partners, opposite partners and diagonal partners), avoids the 'odd person out', and is small enough to allow all to participate. Teams larger than four often do not lead to enough participation.

Pairs are extremely useful. They have the greatest interaction opportunity. Children learn how to share ideas, questions and explanations in a safe, comfortable, format. They can get the confidence from pair discussion to speak out to the larger group. This can be a good stepping- stone to larger group work, as children learn collaborative skills. Pairs can team up into groups of four.

Positive interdependence

Activities need to be designed which *require* children to work together. Individuals need to be connected in such a way that individual success depends on joint effort. The teacher needs to structure activities so that group members have to rely on one another to complete a task. There are a number of ways in which this can be done. Johnson and Johnson (1993) identify nine types of positive interdependence, which teachers should consider in planning the tasks for co-operative learning groups:

- A crucial starting-point for positive interdependence is the development of common *goals*, which must be clearly shared with the groups at the outset, whether that is a product, or a new understanding, or the meeting of specified success criteria. The group must be very clear that they have to work together to achieve a particular shared outcome.

- The use of *resources* is another important factor in creating the conditions where children are required to work interdependently. They are often asked to share materials, or to work separately on related parts of the same piece of work, after which their individual efforts are amalgamated to create a final product. The idea is that the allocation of resources by the teacher is a carefully planned strategy to encourage co-operation.

- The assignment of various different *roles* to the individuals in the group also provides the impetus to work together. These roles would be complementary and interconnected so that children make their own individual, but essential contribution to the work of the whole group. For example: timekeeper, materials manager, encourager, scout, checker.

- The importance of group *identity* has already been mentioned and the creation of team names, logos and mottos encourage children to work together more effectively.

- *Sequence* is another dimension of interdependence which requires the teacher to organise the tasks so that the success of the group's work is dependent on the completion of specific sub tasks in the correct order.

- Scenarios and hypothetical situations allow for the *simulation* of real life situations where children can imagine themselves as part of a team with a related task, which often focuses on the need to clarify values and make decisions.

- *Outside force* can come to bear on the group's need to work together. Competition against the clock is commonly used to encourage more collaborative working, and groups may try to beat their own previous performance. However, generally speaking, competition against others in the class or the school is seen as unhelpful for learning in the model of co-operative learning espoused here.

- *Environmental factors*, especially the physical arrangement for learning are important dimensions of positive interdependence and we have already explored the particular issues around seating arrangements.

- Lastly, *incentives* or celebrations can be used to exert pressure on groups to work together more efficiently. This is not without its problems and any rewards need to be clearly criterion-referenced, as opposed to norm-referenced to avoid the win–lose mentality. All groups should be able to reach the carefully designed criteria and the rewards are available for all who make the appropriate contribution to the group or class task. If teachers want children to become genuinely interdependent, they need to consider the integration of these elements into their plans for learning.

Individual accountability

Co-operative learning groups are not an opportunity for children to avoid work and make less of a contribution. Instead the small-group scenario should make it much harder for less enthusiastic children to disengage than when the teacher is doing all the talking. Although they work as a team, willing to encourage and support each other, each individual child is responsible for their own learning. Teachers need to organise ways of assessing individual performance and of allowing opportunities for children to assess one another, and this fits well with current advice on assessment (such as AifL) Teachers, of course, would be monitoring the group work and can intervene to ask questions of particular individuals. Specific roles can be allocated to focus the work of an individual child and co-operative learning structures can help ensure that individuals are able to make a contribution. For example, random allocation of performance tasks after group work means the group takes responsibility for making sure all can answer questions, explain, etc. In this way the group helps individual members to develop and demonstrate their skills.

Group processing

The group should be asked regularly to self evaluate. They should reflect upon and assess their team's performance /efforts in terms of the academic content of a task as well as their collaborative skills. For this to be effective, there have to be clear success criteria for content and process skills. Groups can then self assess against those criteria. So we need to plan opportunities for children to reflect on social and academic skills in a debriefing session at the end of the lesson. It could be argued that this is one of the most important sections of a lesson, where children are helped to make sense of their learning and comment on their success and failures, and what helped and what hindered them. Yet this is often the most hurried part of lessons at best, or the part which is scrapped if time runs short. Protection of time for the debriefing has to become a key part of classroom management for the teacher encouraging effective co-operative learning. This is facilitated, in part, by the reduction of teacher-talk time implicit in the transformation model of learning. Students should be the ones to sum up the learning – not the teacher. As well as reflecting on and evaluating the group's performance, there would also be the chance to self evaluate and set personal targets:

> At first glance spending time on them may seem too costly. But the reality is quite different. Reflection and planning are essential if students are going to grow in their use of good interpersonal skills and become empowered learners.
>
> (Baloche, 1998, p. 181)

Children need feedback from the teacher on their performance, but if success criteria are clearly defined and shared, then peer and self evaluation become quite straightforward. The provision of written formats to allow children to do this gives them a positive message about the value placed on the activity by the teacher. It has to be taken seriously, and is not simply a question of asking children, 'Do you think you did well today?' or, 'Have you enjoyed the lesson today?' It requires careful consideration of mechanisms to encourage individuals and groups to consider their learning critically. So again, the biggest challenge is to carve out the time for this.

Social skills

Social skills need to be explicitly taught and practised. These need to be defined and assessed. We cannot assume that these important social skills are already in place, so we must develop them alongside curriculum content:

> When students have not been taught how to work with others, teachers should not expect to be able to put them together in groups and have them work together effectively. Teaching students how to work together, teaching them the skills of co-operation is basic – basic not just to the success of co-operative learning . . . – but basic to real life success as well.
>
> (Baloche, 1998, p. 146)

Baloche divides these skills into four subsets: getting into groups, keeping groups staying together and getting the job done, building understanding of academic material and encouraging children to become empowered thinkers. We need to make time for the teaching of these skills in context, so we return to the question of whether the teacher deems them sufficiently important to allocate the time. Children need to know the teacher values these skills as highly as academic skills and gives feedback on them just as systematically. This is a very contentious area for many teachers, who see children's behaviour in groups as a major stumbling-block, which prevents them from using co-operative learning. However these are crucial life-skills which children are not born with, and which seem highly desirable for children to acquire. Why would we not make time to teach them?

There are many examples of the kinds of skills teachers might focus on. For example, using quiet voices, taking turns, sharing materials, moving quietly to groups, disagreeing agreeably, listening actively, encouraging, contributing ideas.

Managing co-operative learning groups

Effective management of a classroom of teams involves quite a number of different skills not necessary in a traditional classroom. The checklist below is designed to helpful:

Co-operative learning management checklist

1. Teachers need to make clear to children:
    - why they will be working in teams
    - the benefits of working with others
    - how long they will be working in this team
    - that ground rules will be needed for working together.

2. Where possible, the room should be arranged so that each child has equal and easy access to each team mate (ideally each one should be able to put both hands on a common piece of paper) and they should be able to easily see the teacher and the blackboard / whiteboard / flip chart.

3. The teacher should establish a quiet signal that at any time quickly focuses all attention from peer interaction to the teacher.

4. Efficient methods of distributing materials should be organised and ground rules agreed which define group and individual responsibilities.

5. A carefully designed task should be set, with clear learning intentions and success criteria. The teacher should always check for understanding of what is expected.

6. Roles and responsibilities should be assigned to children. For example: resources manager, scribe, encourager, timekeeper, etc.

7. Strategies are then used to encourage collaborative approaches to learning (see the list below).

8. While the groups are working, the teacher will use this opportunity to carefully monitor the learning – both academic and social.

9. Evaluation is based on performance of understanding in some format.

10. A debriefing session allows the opportunity for the children to reflect upon their new learning and make connections to what they already know and what they might want to learn next as a result. They should also reflect on the process and their contribution to it.

Co-operative learning structures

A wide range of co-operative learning structures have been developed which can be used in the classroom. Below is a small selection:

Brainstorm

This is a short, time-limited session (2–5 minutes) for all in the team to put down their ideas on a topic or question. The rules here are that all contributions must be valued and written down just as the person says. No judgements are made at this time. The idea is to get down as many ideas as possible.

Brainstorm carousel

This is where the brainstorming is used to cover a number of questions/topics and each team gets the chance to read what others have written and then move on to the next question. Either the groups or the paper can be moved round. When the paper is returned to the start, each group can see what has been added to their original ideas. It is then possible to ask each group to discuss and identify their top 3/4/5 priorities to feed back to the class. This is a good way of gathering a lot of ideas from a whole class into a coherent framework.

Pair discussion

The simplest of all co-operative learning structures is a pair discussion. This provides high levels of participation. Children can be almost anywhere – in rows, on the floor, in their group. Teacher simply says, 'With a partner, talk over …'. This is a good starting-point to get children cued in to the topic.

Think –pair – share

A problem is posed. Children think about it alone for a specified amount of time, then discuss the question with a partner. Children can be called upon to share an answer with the whole class. This means that half the class are actively discussing a question at any one time. Sometimes children are held accountable for listening to their partner because during the share time they are called upon to share the answer they heard from their partner. Problem posed – think time – pair work – share with class.

Numbered heads together

Children in the group number off 1, 2, 3, 4. Teacher asks a question, poses a problem. Children put their heads together to discuss it. Teacher calls a number at random. Child with that number responds. The children have no way of knowing who is going to be asked and so their task is to make sure anyone of their team is able to respond.

Jigsaw

• Divide the lesson content into four segments. For example, if you want children to learn about Martin Luther King, you might divide a short bio-graphy of him into stand-alone segments and assign each child to learn one segment, making they have direct access only to their own segment. Give time to read over their segment at least twice and become familiar with it.

• Form temporary 'expert groups' by having one child from each jigsaw group join other children assigned to the same segment. Give children in these 'expert' groups time to discuss the main points of their segment and to rehearse the presentations they will make to their jigsaw group.

• Bring them back into their jigsaw groups. Ask each one to present his or her segment to the group. Encourage children to find interesting ways of 'teaching' what they know so that others in their group will remember it.

• Move from group to group, observing the process. If any group is having trouble (e.g., a member is dominating or disruptive), make an appropriate intervention.

- At the end of the session, give a quiz on the material so that children quickly come to realize that these sessions are not just fun and games but really count.

Three stray – one stay

If a product is to be shared, after an activity, three members of the team rotate to the next table while Child 1 stays behind to explain the product to the visiting team. After they return, Child 2 then stays behind to explain and the others rotate *two* teams to hear their explanation. Then Child 3 and 4 do the same, rotating *three* and *four* teams ahead. When that is done each child has seen three different products and the team can then discuss differences and use the insights gained to improve their own product. This might be a diagram, a brainstormed list of ideas, a poem, a picture, a flow chart, a poster, etc.

Roam the room

At a signal, each group is asked to send out a scout to view the products of other teams. When they come back they share what they have seen with their group.

Dozens of these structures and strategies aimed at encouraging co-operation and raising the levels of participation in the room are outlined in the co-operative learning literature. This is a very small selection to give a flavour of the methodology. The aim is to develop in the children a sense that it is OK to work together, and that when they collaborate and pool their skills and strengths, they are likely to produce higher quality results. They begin to realise and learn the skills required to work along with others, who may be very different. They find out ,for example, how to negotiate and achieve consensus, how to keep all the team on board and how to make their own contribution to the work of the team. These are important skills and teachers often say it would be difficult for their children to work in this way because they don't have these skills; they don't know how to behave in groups. I argue this is the very reason why children *should* work co-operatively. They need to learn these important skills and we need to teach them explicitly and give them meaningful contexts within which to practise them.

These structures are also highly effective ways of ensuring greater levels of pupil participation. Time spent working this way means more children will be actively involved at any given point in the learning and therefore the retention level is also likely to be higher. This is a move away from teachers standing at the front talking and children sitting in their seats listening (or not!), where levels of participation are traditionally low and often only a few children are engaged in the dialogue the teacher leads from the front.

Evaluation and feedback

A key dimension of the kind of classroom atmosphere being advocated in this book is the increased responsibility for children. 'Effective teaching involves talking regularly with learners about their learning, and listening to them' (SCCC, 1996, p. 18). Really listening to what children have to say alters the power relationships in the classroom and is an important feature of the change required on the part of the teacher. Kohn (1992) cites this changing balance of power and control as one of the main reasons teachers are unsettled by co-operative learning approaches in the classroom: 'There is a certain pleasure to be taken from the role of king or queen, even if one's subjects are very short' (Kohn, 1992, p. 39). In the co-operative learning model, the teacher no longer is the only source of ideas and information; children are encouraged to take on new roles and responsibilities in the learning and so the predictable progression through a planned lesson is not going to be the norm.

Self and peer evaluation

One of the main responsibilities children can usefully take on board is the evaluation of their own and their peers' work. This is possible where there are clear success criteria which allow anyone to examine the piece of work and evaluate it against the set criteria, and is one of the most interesting developments taking place in Scottish primary schools as a result of the use of formative assessment. The sharing of learning intentions, with clear success criteria, often generated in conjunction with the children, has clarified the assessment process for teachers and children alike. It is possible for the teacher to design activities where children take increasing responsibility for assessment and begin to learn for themselves what constitutes a quality piece of work and what would need to be done to improve it.

Paired marking with response partners is one way to regularly involve learners in this kind of evaluation work. Response partners have the task of giving honest feedback on a piece of work, using the success criteria, and offering advice on how they think it could be improved. They are encouraged to give positive feedback first and to give more positives than negatives. This requires a considerable amount of work with children to prepare them to handle these tasks sensitively. They need to explore the ground rules that would make this relationship work: confidentiality, active listening, sensitivity to feelings, and the like. The climate needs to be created where this kind of peer evaluation is routine so that children can develop the skills to evaluate critically their own and others' work. Teachers need to be prepared for a phase when the children's assessment and feedback will be naïve and simplistic. They have to help children learn more sophisticated responses.

However, as with all the changes discussed, the teacher needs to believe that this is a legitimate use of time and children are capable of such self and peer assessment. This is not to say that self and peer assessment replaces the teacher's assessment; the teacher now has a very significant role in providing specific and effective feedback on how to improve performance, rather than spending hours ticking sums and correcting spelling errors. The crucial shift is the changing power relationship, where the children gradually take some control over their own learning, begin to understand their own strengths and weaknesses and are able to think about setting legitimate learning targets for themselves. The endless, helpless reliance on the class teacher as the font of all knowledge is replaced by an approach that empowers learners to take more responsibility for their own progress. Clearly this cannot happen over-night, and children who have no experience of working this way will find it very difficult at the start. As with the teaching of the interpersonal skills required for co-operative group work, these skills need to be carefully taught and practised in meaningful contexts. We cannot just spring this on children and expect to get meaningful responses. Teachers are often disappointed with their first efforts and can give up, concluding that children can't do this kind of thing. Perseverance is essential and, again, that requires faith in the process, in the face of initial disappointments. Teachers have been given lots of sound advice about how this kind of self and peer assessment can be established in the classroom. (Black and Wiliam, 1998a, 1998b; Clarke 2001, 2003, 2005; Smith 2005).

Pupil feedback

The other, perhaps more radical, form of pupil feedback is their evaluation of their experience of learning in the classroom. This requires teachers to be confident enough, not only to examine their own teaching, but to allow the children to do so too. There is no point in asking for feedback and then ignoring it or, worse, taking the children to task for giving their honest appraisal. The feedback has to be valued. Brookfield (1995) advocates this as one of the key lenses through which we must view our teaching if we are to be genuinely critical in our reflection. This kind of feedback helps us see our teaching through the students' eyes, alerting us to problems and pointing us in the direction of changes we might make. It lets us see how differently children can experience the same lesson and, importantly, how different any of those interpretations can be from our original intentions.

There are many strategies teachers can use and, as with the evaluation activities mentioned above, careful preparation with the children is essen-tial. Because of the existing power relationships in the class, there are many possible challenges in this endeavour, from children telling teachers exactly what they think they want to hear, through to telling them exactly what they think they don't want to hear. Clearly an atmosphere of trust and mutual respect in the classroom will be significant and this climate needs to exist for successful evaluation to take place. The irony is that the very process of seeking out the opinions of children, and acting upon them, will help to build that trust and respect. We return yet again to the dilemma faced by teachers whose own beliefs and values lead them to be inherently suspicious of taking children's opinions seriously.

In the current climate of increasing rights for children and apparently increasing vulnerability for teachers, it is easy to dismiss the rights of the child by coming up with clear examples where teachers may feel they have abused those rights and lacked any sense of responsibility. But it is possible to argue that the best way to teach responsible citizenship is to act it out in our everyday dealings with children. It can also be built into teaching methodologies in the ways outlined in this chapter to give young people the opportunities to develop the relevant skills and dispositions in a meaningful context. It doesn't seem sensible to advocate the need for children to become more responsible while perpetuating a system which formalises their lack of power and choice. Teachers can be on the receiving end of pupils' frustration at their limited influence over what happens to them at school, and the last area I'd like to explore in this chapter is the ways in which teachers encourage responsible and caring behaviour within a classroom that is a learning community.

Community or compliance?

Kohn (1999) explored the difference between what he would describe as bribes and threats to get children to behave, and encouraging them to take responsibility for their own behaviour towards others. There is not space in this book to go into detail about the whole area of handling children's behaviour and the conflicting philosophies which underpin the various approaches used in schools. However, it seems important to flag up the important issues relating to building community. Kohn's ideas match well with the idea of working towards to creating the kind of climate where children behave reasonably because they feel some sense of personal and collective responsibility rather than because they want to get a reward or please the teacher. Rewards and sanctions may work in the short term and are highly seductive for teachers looking for solutions to complex behaviour problems, and to be honest, trying to survive in sometimes difficult classrooms. However they are less successful in the longer term, when the children are not in school, not with the teacher, not getting the rewards. When good teachers organise their classrooms from a mindset where children are not to be trusted, they will automatically devise control mechanisms which seem necessary to survive. This may include very tight organisation and control of resources, minimal movement around the classroom, very clearly laid out rewards and sanctions to control behaviour, and an overall sense of the teacher being completely in charge of how things happen in the classroom. The aim is to minimise the opportunities for disruptive behaviour and allow the learning to take place. This strategy of 'keeping a tight lid on the class' is ironically the very one which may militate against real learning. Pupils are cast in the role of helpless learners who can only progress under the watchful eye of the teacher. They constantly defer to the teacher's superior knowledge and work on carefully timetabled activities and tasks which keep them busy at their desks. The opportunity to raise questions, make a contribution, relate the learning to their own experience, or genuinely reflect on their learning is often missing. There is a dearth of activities that allow learners to make sense of new ideas and connect them to existing knowledge and understanding. The children often spend a lot of time working out or guessing what the teacher is 'looking for', rather than exploring ideas for themselves. Classes organised along these lines appear to be very efficient, with pupils often busy 'working'. However it may be worth considering the extent to which there is merely an illusion of learning in such classrooms. Children are busy 'doing', but are they busy 'learning'? The two are not necessarily the same thing.

For some teachers, in some schools, with some age groups, such a controlling approach may work well. However, as a long-term strategy, especially with challenging pupils, it is unlikely to be fruitful. It is based on notions of inequality and power. The ethos created will eat away at mutually respectful relationships. It is unhelpful in promoting the real sense of responsibility in young people so desired in society. The one-sided nature of the relationship seems unlikely to develop independent thinkers who ask questions, have opinions of their own and are used to having those opinions taken seriously. If we are concerned with creating responsible citizens, we need to consider a longer-term approach to encouraging our children to behave with consideration for others.

This means examining the whole experience we have together in school, including the environment we set up, and thinking about how it could be different. It means a paradigm shift from the teacher at the centre, working out ways of 'getting children to behave', to the child at the centre and the teacher helping to create a real community of learners with the qualities and capacities to care and contribute to society. We need to think about the ways in which we can encourage and develop those qualities and empower children to make good choices and decisions about how to interact with others. The nature of the curriculum on offer is equally important. It is much more likely that difficult situations will arise when children are struggling to see the relevance of the curriculum and when the teaching methods used result in little involvement or engagement with the learning. When children feel they have no say or choice in any of the decisions that affect them every day, they are also more likely to present difficult behaviour. Key to the problem would seem to be the explicit discussion of how we treat one another and why we should treat other others with respect and care. This requires quite demanding and time-consuming work with children, over a sustained period of time and in a learning community where they feel safe and valued. The teacher has a great deal of influence in the creation of this climate and considerable power in determining the parameters for the discussion.

In Chapter 5 we will explore the ways in which teachers and trainee teachers can be supported to use that influence to good effect.

Chapter 5

DISCUSSION AND RECOMMENDATIONS

This final chapter discusses the implications of the issues raised in the last four chapters. I have examined the current policy context in Scotland and argued that it may provide conditions that are conducive to real change in relation to the way we organise learning in the primary classroom. I have also explored the nature of that possible change, not only in relation to pedagogy, but also in relation to the climate created for learning. This has involved the exploration of the professional self of teachers and the ways in which their beliefs and values about learners and learning impact on their teaching. Given the centrality of the teacher in creating the conditions for effective learning within a caring, learning community, I now want to explore the issues around initial teacher education, teachers' continuing professional development and make recommendations in relation to both.

Although the current policy context in Scotland is important in legitimising new approaches to teaching and learning, I believe the biggest impact on changing teachers' motivation to work towards creating a learning community will come in practice from more widespread implementation of co-operative learning methodology used effectively by individual teachers in classrooms. Thus, exposure to high quality, long-term training and support in co-operative learning can lead teachers to reconceptualise their teaching in this way. The implementation of the basic elements outlined in Chapter 4 can encourage teachers to reappraise their role as teacher and consider instead the facilitation and design skills needed to organise this kind of learning. The approach allows teachers to explore the benefits of higher levels of participation and active involvement of children in their learning. Experience of co-operative learning structures that promote increased responsibility in children, both academically and socially, open up possibilities for teachers to consider the effects of such changes. They allow teachers to entertain the possibility of moving away from an emphasis on competition, individualism and transmission teaching to judge the benefits of equality, collaboration and transformation in the classroom. Of course, the process of such fundamental change in practice is fraught with potential difficulties and these are discussed below, but I argue that high quality, long-term staff development and support in co-operative learning may be the most significant strategy that could be employed to deliver learning communities in our schools.

Initial teacher education

Clearly there are enormous implications for the education of new teachers. It would be important for Teacher Education Institutions (TEIs) to adopt a similar approach to learning and teaching as is advocated for schools; indeed it is possible to argue that they should be in the vanguard of new developments in learning and teaching. Teacher education could be more closely connected with the principles of A Curriculum for Excellence, encouraging those same key capacities in newly qualified teachers: confident individuals, successful learners, effective contributors, responsible citizens. The underlying principles of formative assessment could be more rigorously applied in this setting, and co-operative learning approaches could be incorporated into methodology, offering not only effective learning and teaching strategies, but the opportunity for students to experience the approach first hand.

It may be that the Scottish Teachers for a New Era project (online resource, 2006) at Aberdeen University will offer opportunities to introduce different approaches to learning and teaching. This project draws on a similar initiative in the USA (Teachers for a New Era online resource, 2006) where teacher education is being restructured in a number of institutions. One of the main aims of the project is to equip Scottish teachers to support learners in the twenty-first century and contribute to improving learning. Peter Peacock, the then Scottish Minister for Education and Young People, welcomed the emphasis on 'the importance of research-based practice both in initial teacher education and in teaching' (SEED, 2005, p. 11). The research base for co-operative learning is considerable and worthy of exploration in this context, where there is a unique opportunity to examine the methodology used in initial teacher education and make changes in the future.

One current example of this way of working is to be found in the Professional Studies element of the Professional Graduate Diploma in Education (Primary) at the University of Glasgow. Co-operative learning techniques, and the philosophy behind them have been gradually introduced into the Professional Studies component of this one-year course since 2002.

The course philosophy is firmly based on constructivist approaches to learning and teaching and this is modelled in tutorials. Richardson (1997) argues for a more constructivist approach to teacher education, where we are seen to practise what we preach. She points out that students generally come to teacher education with a transmission view of teaching, and suggests a number of strategies to address this, including detailed debriefing of school experience and the use of reflective writing in journals to promote deeper thinking and to gauge understanding. These strategies have been adopted in Professional Studies. The aim of the course is to build on the experience of student teachers on school placements and in faculty, modelling the importance of the constructivist learning which we so readily advocate they use in their own teaching, and how that impacts on the actions they take in the classroom.

This course is based on a democratic notion of respecting the learners as individuals, while at the same time recognising the value of a collaborative learning community. We examine together the experience of students and challenge their notions of what it is to be a 'teacher' and a 'learner'. We recognise the emotional dimension of teaching and the enormous investment of self in the process. An important part of the course is therefore aimed at exploring students' experiences, values, beliefs and assumptions in relation to learning and teaching.

Students are actively involved in making meaning, processing and relating information to their own experience through dialogue and collaboration. There is an emphasis on understanding and the learner's increasing responsibility for his or her own learning. This reflects an holistic view of learners which takes account of the emotional aspects of learning.

Co-operative, experiential learning is modelled and explicitly discussed in tutorials, providing students with concrete ideas about the strategies they will be expected to put into practice on school experience. Group work is rigorously planned, promoting definition of roles, individual accountability and performance of understanding. Design terminology is explored and quality criteria for both product and process are made clear, often in negotiation with students. Debriefing of sessions helps students to make sense of their learning and make connections to other learning. We make efforts to build a community of learners in each tutorial group where students can feel supported in their learning over the year. Ground rules for how we treat one another are developed at the beginning of the course. These are a working set of guidelines, which are amended over the course of the year, based on experience. We aim to involve students actively in the learning and to create the kind of atmosphere in the class where learning is enjoyable as well as effective. We hope to see a parallel approach to creating a collaborative learning community with children on school placements.

Evaluations of this approach to teacher education have been largely very positive and students have valued the emphasis on experiencing the methodology as part of their own learning. We have seen increasing numbers of students become confident enough to try to implement the strategies modelled in tutorials, and have now moved to including the requirement to carry out a series of co-operative learning lessons in the remit for the final school placement of the course. Recent policy initiatives, outlined above, have made it easier for us to persuade sometimes sceptical, student teachers that these approaches to learning and teaching are highly relevant in the twenty-first century. It became increasingly clear to us that it is essential to convince PGDE students of the research evidence underpinning the approach and we have made this very explicit. However, our work in faculty was often hampered by the lack of examples of practice in this methodology and by the response students sometimes received in schools when they tried to implement co-operative learning. This situation is gradually changing as more schools are influenced by the AifL initiative and are routinely giving children more opportunities to work together. The framework for A Curriculum for Excellence also adds legitimacy to the endeavour and students are more likely to come back to faculty reporting that their teachers are using some the approaches we are advocating. More importantly, these changes in methodology are clearly in line with major national initiatives and less easily dismissed as a whim of out-of-touch university staff.

There is cause for cautious optimism here arising out of the influence of the three factors: the validity given to alternative approaches to learning and teaching through A Curriculum for Excellence, the shift in thinking due to the research and practice associated with the Assessment is for Learning initiative, and exposure to co-operative learning philosophy and techniques. I have experienced this change in climate over the course of the last four years and, as far as our work on the course above is concerned, it has been a positive development. It has become increasingly easy to persuade student teachers about the case for co-operative learning, and early analysis of the data from last year's cohort points to their ability to make the connections between these initiatives. We have done much more detailed work with students this year on AifL and the connections with co-operative learning methodologies have become apparent. The legitimate interest in formative assessment strategies, out there in the schools they visit, has opened a door to co-operative learning for students who want to try out the methodology. It has meant that students have been much more likely to see practice that chimes with the approaches we are advocating in faculty, and this has reduced the suspicion many had about what they perceived to be unusual teaching methods. Many more students now have experience of pair work, group work, and self and peer evaluation in real classrooms, with real children to reflect upon and share when they return from school placements. In the ensuing discussions more students can call on a wider range of experience, which can be much more easily related to the theoretical frameworks explored in faculty. As we continue to develop our approach to supporting students in developing their understanding of teaching and learning and their own important role in the process, we hope to improve the preparation of our newly qualified teachers for teaching in the twenty-first century. It has been important to have a course philosophy, to justify it with sound research evidence, and to encourage the development of an informed professional stance, through critical reflection. We encourage our students to become teachers who ask questions, have good theoretical understanding as well as practical skill, are well informed, can justify their choices of approaches to teaching and learning, and recognise the importance of reflection.

This involves much greater use of all of the teaching methodologies outlined previously in this book designed to encourage self-awareness as well as individual and collective responsibility. The most common instructional strategy in universities has been the lecture, which we know to be one of the least effective strategies in terms of engagement and subsequent retention. There are a number of ways in which the methodologies used in teacher education could be more closely aligned with those practices expected of twenty-first century teachers. Adopting a model of co-operative learning with student teachers is a tried and tested approach. Modelling successful learning and teaching approaches should be a central plank of teacher education courses throughout Scotland.

Induction

However well we might try to prepare students in TEIs, the transition from student teacher to qualified teacher can be a challenging one. Alongside the excitement and anticipation of finally getting the freedom of having their own class, newly qualified teachers are naturally apprehensive about the responsibility that lies ahead and how they will settle into their new role. Much has been written about the experience of induction in the UK (Tickle, 2000; Bubb, 2001) and in the Scottish context (Martin and Rippon, 2005; Rippon and Martin, 2006a; Draper *et al.*, 1992, 2004; Draper and O'Brien, 2006). There are particular issues around the need to fit in and conform which are of particular relevance here. Where newly qualified teachers see conformity to school norms as crucial to their survival, they are unlikely to experiment with new teaching methodologies, especially if they are frowned on by the school. It is certainly the case that student teachers on school placement feel constrained in their approaches to learning and teaching by the prevailing culture in the school, and the particular pedagogical practices of the class teacher. It is an emotional imperative for most new teachers to gain acceptance from their colleagues.

There is much evidence in the literature of the new teacher's need to fit in with the ethos of the school (Hargreaves and Woods, 1984; Nias *et al.*, 1989). Hayes (2001) describes it as a process of 'enculturation' where student teachers assimilate the prevailing values of the new school. He calls it 'strategic compliance'. In studies of the induction experience (Martin and Rippon, 2003, 2005; Rippon and Martin, 2003, 2006a, 2006b), newly qualified teachers have highlighted the importance for them of the power relationship they have with their induction supporter. Some mentioned the need to conform in their first year and fit in at all costs:

We all want jobs at the end of it because it's a probation year. We have to keep quiet.

For me the first year is about conforming to the school ethos.

(Martin and Rippon, 2003)

The system of new teacher induction is, of course, part of a process of socialisation which aids the assimilation of new teachers into the culture of the school (Lortie, 1975; Hargreaves and Woods, 1984). It helps them to assume the values and behaviours accepted by the dominant culture of the school. In other words, the socialisation process and the professional culture perpetuate existing beliefs, standards and practices and impact on the long-term performance of the novice teacher (Feiman-Nemser, 1983; Huling-Austin, 1990). Smith (2001) suggests that the induction tutor or supporter becomes the gatekeeper to the profession. Conforming to the gatekeeper's vision of a good teacher is essential in the probationer teacher's pursuit of full registration, even if this is not a desirable goal for the probationer teacher or the profession. This power relationship, where the probationer is seen as an apprentice to the experienced teacher, encourages new teachers to conform to existing practices, whilst prohibiting the development of new approaches and regeneration of the profession. (Rippon and Martin, 2006a).

There is, therefore, a considerable amount of work to be done in TEIs to prepare novice teachers to able to cope with the 'enculturation' process in school. There is a need for a clearer emphasis on establishing a professional and personal stance which has been considered carefully from a number of different perspectives, and upon which probationer teachers can draw in their early teaching career. Schools, of course, can help enormously by creating the kind of learning community we've been discussing, where newly qualified teachers would feel safe and secure enough to experiment and grow professionally. More work could usefully be done with mentors and school managers to explore these issues.

Continuing professional development

Research evidence warns us of the potential difficulties in training and supporting experienced teachers in new instructional strategies, many of which have already been identified in previous chapters. Despite the extensive research to validate co-operative learning and demonstrate its advantages – the ability to accommodate diversity, the emphasis on social and academic skills, and the link with social constructivism – Antil et al. (1998) suggest that several questions remain about its implementation in classrooms. In their study of 85 elementary school teachers in the US, they found that although 93% of participants reported the use of co-operative learning, only small numbers of teachers were actually using the structured approaches advocated by the research. The vast majority modified and adapted the procedures, so that many of the specific elements required for effectiveness were omitted. Teachers were positive about the benefits of the methodology, yet failed to implement it according to recommended models.

A study of the Critical Skills Programme (Baron *et al.*, 2004) found that although teachers were extremely positive about the CSP model, most were implementing only isolated elements of the overall approach, and were not sufficiently steeped in the model to radically alter their teaching. Cherry-picking attractive elements of any new methodology is always a possibility when busy teachers are exposed to limited, short-term staff development opportunities. There was no intent to subvert the implementation of the methodology, just a limited understanding of its underlying philosophy, often as a result of insufficient training. The adoption of a whole new approach to teaching requires systematic and sustained support over a period of time, if the hearts and minds of teachers are to be engaged in ways that challenge their existing paradigm and persuade them that the new approach should be used in its entirety and become an integral part of their teaching repertoire.

Lopata *et al.* (2003) found similar results when examining the self-reported use of co-operative learning with teachers in suburban elementary and middle schools in western New York State. These teachers were considered to have advanced knowledge and skills and yet reported that their use of co-operative learning was less than expected. The authors attributed this to a range of possible factors: increased pressure to meet academic standards through testing, class size, and student behaviour problems. If teachers who have advanced knowledge and skills are still challenged to find time to implement co-operative learning, we must consider the reasons why. The list above corresponds with some of the concerns of teachers outlined in Chapter 1, not least the pressure to raise attainment, however, what is not addressed here is the extent of the teachers' commitment to the methodology. Is it possible that when teachers have really bought into the philosophy of co-operative learning, they will make time to fit it in, regardless of the external pressures, because they are convinced of its effectiveness?

Lopata *et al.* (2003) suggest that teachers need to be made aware of the range of co-operative learning models and methods, as well as the potential difficulties, before attempting to put the models into practice. Staff development opportunities are again highlighted as important in this respect, with sustained follow-up support in schools. Veenman *et al.* (2000) found that primary school teachers in their study in the Netherlands were not implementing the elements of co-operative learning regarded as essential for co-operation. Most of the teachers did not use a specific approach and spent little time teaching teamwork skills. Basic elements were not addressed by the teachers. Emmer and Gerwels (2002) observed the lessons of 18 elementary school teachers in seven schools in a large urban school district in the US over the course of a year. They found that teachers, all of whom were experienced in the use of co-operative learning, did not usually adhere to any particular model: notably missing were individual accountability to the group, formal systems of testing and group rewards based on individual performance, the allocation of roles, and group assignments in lessons. These are major omissions, which betray a lack of understanding of and/or commitment to the model. 'This suggests that experienced teachers can and do modify co-operative learning to fit their beliefs, goals, and classroom conditions' (Emmer et al., 2002, p. 89).

The adaptation of new methodology to fit teachers' own ways of working and thinking is an interesting dimension of staff development. Translation of a 'pure' model of any instructional strategy into practice in the classroom is clearly not going to happen. Teachers will always adapt and change methodologies to fit their own preferences; teaching is a very personal and individual endeavour, so it is to be expected that teachers will automatically mould new practices to suit their own particular style. The problems arise when they change it so radically that it becomes unrecognisable, either because they have been very selective in their use of the isolated strategies, or have altered the strategies so much they no longer serve the same purpose. The dangers then are considerable: their version of the strategies may be less effective than the researched approach; teachers may reject the new approach altogether because their particular version of it has not been successful; they may be under the misapprehension that what they are doing constitutes the new approach, when it fact it doesn't actually fulfil the criteria.

These challenges arise with the introduction of any new methodology, but for co-operative learning the underlying philosophy is at the heart of the matter. In many ways, the sum of the parts of co-operative learning does not constitute the whole. As a vehicle to assist in the creation of learning community, it is not just an instructional strategy with a series of neat structures to follow; it is a major change in the way we think about organising learning. It is not simply a matter of tinkering with our practice; it is a radical transformation of the teaching and learning process, which requires a similar shift in the role of teacher and pupils. Therefore the level of implementation is a crucial indicator of the extent to which teachers have assimilated the philosophy and not just the techniques.

Krol et al. (2001) highlight the important role of the teacher and the central place of training: 'Successful implementation of co-operative learning largely depends on teachers' understanding of what co-operative learning really is and their capacity to apply the methods insightfully and appropriately' (p. 39). In their study of a staff development programme, the researchers presented co-operative learning as a philosophical and practical approach and observed encouraging training effects in their sample of elementary teachers. This training programme was based on research, and tailored to a long-term approach to implementation of co-operative learning. The teachers' levels of expertise and experience, including a sound conceptual understanding of the methodology, were significant and must be taken into account when evaluating the implementation of this kind of approach to learning and teaching.

Johnson *et al.* (2000) highlight the need for the teacher to have this conceptual understanding of the whole approach. They point to the long- term benefits of such an understanding of methodology and its resulting transferability to other contexts, as it becomes part of a teacher's repertoire. Their recommendations involve in-depth training, which they recommend should span at least three years:

- *Pre-training*, where the conditions for co-operative learning are established in the classroom
- *Training* in the conceptual framework and practical procedures
- *Post training*, where on-going support is given to embed the strategies.

Eraut points to the added difficulty for experienced teachers of having to unlearn existing practices:

> Changing one's teaching style involves deskilling, risk, information overload and mental strain as more and more gets treated as problematic and less and less is taken for granted.
>
> (Eraut, 1994, p. 36)

Therefore, the emotional plight of experienced teachers should be attended to in professional development strategies to support them in making the necessary transition in their teaching approach. The importance of coaching in context for the sustained delivery of change in teachers' practices is highlighted by Joyce and Showers. They identify five ways in which coaching contributes to the transfer of training:

- Coached teachers generally practise new strategies more frequently.
- They use newly learned strategies more appropriately.
- They exhibit greater long-term retention of knowledge and skill.
- They are more likely to explain the new approaches to their students so that they understand the purpose of the strategies being used.
- They exhibit clearer cognitions with regard to the purposes and uses of the new strategies.

(Joyce and Showers, 1988, p. 89)

Joyce and Showers argue that the evidence supports two working hypotheses on which effective training can be based:

- Demonstration, practice with feedback and the study of the rationale of the strategy will provide an initial skill level.
- Extensive practice is required to transfer the model into the teaching repertoire. Without coaching this extended practice is unlikely to take place.

Reeves *et al.* (2001) highlight the need to internalise the changes in professional practice: 'The key to improving performance becomes successfully supporting a process of "sense making" by learners that will make the new practice professionally and personally meaningful' (p. 209). But they also recognise that there is a social process involved in implementing successful change in schools. Merely engaging individual teachers in a new pedagogy is not sufficient. A supporting social network is essential. If all the teachers working in a particular school are on the same journey of learning, the mutual exchange of experience, the feeling that others are facing similar challenges and that there is time for reflection, constitute a powerful mechanism for the continuing growth and development of new pedagogies.

Such a long-term, in-depth, teacher-centred approach to training is uncommon. Staff in the study of CSP (Baron *et al.*, 2004) identified a number of conditions which they felt would contribute to effective implementation:

- all staff in a school should be trained
- local training should be made available
- more time to digest and reflect upon the ideas in the model
- a structured process of gradual induction into the methodology
- more opportunity to come together with other teachers to plan, prepare and support one another
- co-operative teaching to provide in-class support
- collaboration within schools
- suitable materials – a bank of challenges
- management support to ensure continuity and progression.

The research referred to above warns us of the many difficulties involved in persuading teachers to change their pedagogy in quite fundamental ways. It also gives us a range of possible strategies to combat such difficulties.

The training for co-operative learning routinely offered in Scotland takes the form of a three- day course, often with a follow-up day. Network Educational Press have a three-day follow-up course and also offer a second level of training, typically lasting for a further three days. Although in-house, designer training sessions are available for CSP, much of the training is delivered in open institutes, to groups of individual teachers from different schools and local authorities. These courses are well subscribed, with a maximum of 25 on a course, and hundreds of teachers have now completed the training.

North Lanarkshire Education Department's courses are part of a local authority initiative aimed at training all their teachers in co-operative learning. The training is organised in larger groups, typically around 60 in each academy. In an effort to roll out the model, they have put in place development officers who work in schools alongside teachers and assist with training. In both cases, the training has been done by external trainers from the US and Canada, although Network Educational Press have a clear system to induct new, local trainers into the programme on offer. North Lanarkshire has similarly used the skills of the Canadian trainers to support and develop a local model, where staff can be supported from within the resources of the local authority.

There is clear support in the literature for a much more systematic, longer-term approach to the training and support of teachers in co-operative learning, if it is to be properly implemented. I support that approach but also argue for a change in the nature of that training. I have adapted the Johnson *et al.* (2000) three-stage process as a framework for change in what follows.

Pre-training

The need to understand the conceptual framework that underpins this approach to learning and teaching is fundamental and that doesn't happen in a three-day course where the emphasis is on learning about the key features of co-operative learning and the teaching strategies. I am therefore arguing for training that is also focused firmly on the theoretical and research basis for co-operative learning and is explicit about the links between the benefits identified in the literature and the models advocated by the research. These are crucial links for teachers to make if they are to come an understanding of the reasons *why* this approach is effective and, importantly, to be in a position to judge how it fits in with or challenges their own views about how learning should be organised. Because it is so radically different to traditional class teaching, and to the experience of most teachers, co-operative learning can be seen by some as a bit 'off the wall', so it is important to ground the practice in theory for teachers and use this as one way to help convince them of its effectiveness. The research evidence base for the effectiveness of co-operative learning is so sound that it seems sensible that we should start with this information. The more we can do to help teachers understand the philosophy underpinning the approach, the more likely they are to see the possibilities for their own teaching.

It may be useful then for teachers to be asked to do some reading before they attend any training course. We are dealing with professional people who are capable of absorbing and analysing theoretical frameworks and reviewing research. There is no reason why the main ideas related to the underlying philosophy of co-operative learning could not be presented in a straightforward format and provided for teachers to read in advance. Careful selection of Internet websites could also provide fundamental information about the approach in advance of the training. In this way, we would avoid the scenario where teachers turn up for a co-operative learning course wondering what they have let themselves in for. Many teachers are apprehensive about what for some is a quite threatening 'informal' approach to training where they are not passively reading the Power Point presentation along with the trainer, but are required to participate in ways that they may find initially challenging. We would not spring the methodology on children without explaining what was going on and why, and we should not do it with teachers. In Chapter 4, I suggested that teachers need to prepare children for a change of methodology by making it very clear why they will be working in this different way and, importantly the benefits of working with others. This is a crucial prerequisite for teachers too, and more time could usefully be spent on preparing them to be ready to engage with the ideas.

During the actual training sessions, there are many ways that co-operative learning structures could be used to allow teachers the opportunity to dip into the theoretical frameworks and learn about the research on co-operative learning, so that they would be exposed to both the theory and practice at the same time. The content used to experience the process of co-operative learning could usefully be the theoretical foundation of the approach and the research evidence of its many benefits. This approach to training may also lead teachers to go on to read more for themselves and gain a progressively deeper understanding of what they are doing and why.

Training

Evaluations of the training provided for co-operative learning in Scotland would indicate that it is generally of a high standard and the modelling of the process is well done by experienced and able trainers. Materials are routinely provided to give support to teachers when they go back to school, and the experiential nature of the sessions make them powerful and challenging staff development opportunities. I argue for training to be, in addition, much more explicit in addressing the bigger picture of the change that is required of teachers. It should not focus almost exclusively on techniques and strategies, but should concentrate more on the fundamental shift in approach that this involves for the teacher and the children.

Co-operative learning is essentially a democratic approach to learning and teaching, and training should be more transparent in addressing the ideological issues involved. We have looked in previous chapters at the personal and professional stance of the teacher, and it is important that this crucial area is addressed more specifically in training. There is no point in pretending that this is only about a few changes to a teacher's teaching methods or to the way a teacher organises group work: it is a fundamental change in the power relationships in the classroom and it would be helpful to be more transparent about that. Therefore, as well as exploring the benefits for children's learning, there should also be opportunity to explore the implications for the teacher. Some teachers may not view the changes as benefits for them personally and professionally and this dilemma needs to be examined in the training. Co-operative learning is not a value-free approach to teaching: teachers need to be given time and space to reflect on their own beliefs and values, and this should be part of staff development.

There are many co-operative learning structures available to allow teachers to work in this way, in non-threatening small groups, to explore their reactions with colleagues. This is important work on the inner terrain of the teacher mentioned in previous chapters, and we should not ignore this important aspect of change when designing training. It is not easy to tackle these very sensitive areas with teachers, where their personal, and often deeply held, beliefs are involved. Trainers have not only to be skilled and knowledgeable in co-operative learning, but need the conviction and passion to be able to challenge and support teachers in examining their belief systems.

For some teachers, of course, co-operative learning will be a joyous discovery: a structure and validation for all that they have always believed in about children's education, and they will find it fairly easy to incorporate it into their practice. They will see connections to many of the strategies they use already and will welcome the rigour and definition the approach provides to collaborative child-centred education. For others, the journey to co-operative learning will be a more complex one, where they have to confront their own beliefs about learning and learners, and make choices about how they will teach. And for some, this way of working will be beyond the pale, will not fit in with anything they value in teaching and will be rejected at a fairly early stage.

It is because of the wide range of reactions to the ideas involved that it is important to explore the many different dilemmas faced by teachers and give them time to reflect. Therefore, I argue, we should be working from the inside out with teachers on this crucial dimension of co-operative learning, and not training in technique alone. Palmer (1998) makes an important distinction between teachers making real connections with learners and putting technique into practice: 'technique is what teachers use until the real teacher arrives' (p. 5). Time needs to be made available to teachers to explore these fundamental issues and it is also helpful to engage in that discussion with trainers who are experienced in co-operative learning.

Post-training

There is, it seems, little or no chance of significant long-term change unless on-going support is in put place. Where teachers are trained for relatively short periods of time, with a focus almost entirely on technique, and then essentially left to their own devices, there is less chance of them persevering with the approach, far less changing their views about the way learning is organised in the classroom. Teachers seem to be well aware of the need for on-going training and support and in the CSP study (Baron *et al.*, 2004) they themselves named their list of requirements for the successful implementation of the new approach. If we are seriously concerned about implementing co-operative learning, we need to acknowledge the needs of practitioners as they grapple with new methodology; support networks, coaching, continuing training opportunities, and space and time to reflect on their teaching seem to be essential features of post-training.

Support networks seem to be a crucial long-term element in the engagement of teachers with new methodology (Palmer, 1998; Brookfield, 1995; Wiliam and Thompson, 2006; Joyce and Showers, 1988; Reeves *et al.*, 2001). Access to peer support to discuss teaching and learning, and – most importantly – the challenges being faced in the classroom, is an important element of the support package, especially when teachers are being asked to radically alter their usual patterns of teaching and interacting with children. The uncertainty which results from such change has been discussed in previous chapters and is particularly the case when teachers are in that space where they know that what they are trying to do is worthwhile, but haven't yet quite mastered the practice. The limbo between having left behind the comfortable skill levels you had with your previous approach, and feeling like a novice in the new methodology, is where the support is most required. We need to hear that other teachers are experiencing the same dip in confidence, that it is normal and that it will change. The opportunity to discuss these legitimate fears about apparent lack of expertise allows teachers to put their feelings into perspective and give them the self-assurance to continue. The sense of belonging to a community of teacher learners inspires confidence and encourages perseverance.

These communities can be set up within a school, with individual teachers coming together to discuss their practice. School management may facilitate such meetings, and obviously this is the best option, where time is protected for the important work of sharing ideas and practice. However, teachers may need to seek out like- minded colleagues and set up their own support network if they do not find themselves in that fortunate position. Clearly, if local or national support mechanisms are available for teachers and schools to tap into, as with the Assessment is for Learning initiative, then it is far easier for teachers to develop their skills and understanding in a more systematic way. Access to web networks makes this an easier prospect than ever to manage for isolated teachers.

Coaching in context has been used with success in other initiatives, for example, in Glasgow with Early Intervention (SOED, 1998) and Teaching for Effective Learning (Glasgow City Council online resource, 2003). To support the Early Intervention initiative, pre-5 and primary staff in Glasgow primary teachers received training from seconded staff working directly with them on reading and numeracy teaching in their own schools. A locally organised approach, using central funding, allowed large numbers of teachers to be supported in context, directly affecting the learning of even larger numbers of young children. In tackling Teaching for Effective Learning, Glasgow used their additional probationary staff to release experienced teachers to work as coaches in 21 different clusters. The coaches were trained and supported centrally and then charged with supporting teachers to develop specific approaches to teaching in the classroom.

It seems highly desirable when asking for such root and branch change in the classroom that we offer in-class support to teachers, as well as training courses. Glasgow City Council Education Department is a good example of a local authority that organised its resources to utilise central funding to meet local authority priorities, through the use of coaches trained in particular areas of learning and teaching. North Lanarkshire Education Department has begun to organise its own on-going support for the implementation of co-operative learning on a local authority basis. This has involved the secondment of a Co-operative Learning Co-ordinator who has come from Canada with a considerable track record in training in co-operative learning. Six development officers have also been seconded to work in schools, coaching and supporting staff. The department are seeking whole system change, aiming to train and support all of their 5,000 teaching staff.

Time for reflection and review seems to be very difficult for teachers to create for themselves. The nature of the work they do leaves them with little time for much more than preparation and planning for the next round of teaching. The benefits of reflection on practice have already been discussed and seem to far outweigh the disadvantages of having to find the time to do it. Covey (1998) calls it 'sharpening the saw' and argues that if we don't take time to stand back and consider renewal strategies, we are in danger of burning out. He likens it to a woodcutter refusing to stop to sharpen a blunt saw as he works very hard at cutting down a tree; the reason he gives is that he is far too busy sawing to stop: this is clearly very short-sighted. Teachers need to take time out from teaching to get clearer about what they are doing, why and whether it's working: it's equally short-sighted of them to think that they couldn't stop teaching long enough to reflect on their teaching. The process of reflection also allows the opportunity to put concerns about professional practice into perspective. This is particularly the case when the reflection is shared with colleagues working in a similar context, as discussed in Chapter 3.

It would be useful in the follow up to training on co-operative learning to have structured opportunities for participants to engage in some kind of reflective writing as they experiment back in their classrooms with the methodology. Moon (1999, 2004) advocates the use of learning journals as a mechanism for this kind of reflection, which prepares students to view knowledge and situations as problematic and socially constructed, rather than as certain or absolute truths. This is a hard lesson to learn in the demanding, practical context of teaching where clear-cut, right or wrong, answers might feel more immediately comforting.

Structured journal writing would be a way of teachers keeping in touch with their reactions as they make changes to their practice and provide a focus for discussion in support networks or on follow up training days. There is much in the literature to back up the idea that the actual process of writing in itself is a catalyst for reflection (Hoover, 1994) allowing the writer the opportunity to stand back from the experience and consider it more objectively. Emig (1977) cites many attributes of writing which support learning: for example, the ability to revise ideas, a sharper focus through the deliberate choice of words and the active nature of the process. Most training is organised so that there is a space between sessions to put the ideas into practice, and structured journal writing in the intervening weeks could concentrate the participants' attention on their developing skills, the successes and challenges they have faced, and the ways in which they have tackled those challenges.

I believe that the model of training and support outlined above would increase the chance of successful implementation of co-operative learning in practice and therefore the probability of moving towards the creation of a genuine learning community. However, there are many reasons why, even with high quality long-term training and support, teachers may still resist taking that final step towards shifting the learning relationships and balance of power in the classroom.

The bigger picture

Panitz (2000) cites the emphasis in the education system on individualism and competition, memorisation of content and individual performance as major reasons for teachers to be reticent about adopting co-operative learning as their preferred instructional strategy. He points to the fact that most teachers will themselves have been taught by traditional methods, which will have impacted on their view of learning and teaching. In his analysis of reasons for teachers' reticence he lists, among others: lack of appropriate prepared materials for use in the classroom, concern with teacher evaluation, students' resistance to the techniques, lack of teacher training in co-operative learning methods, large classes and inappropriate classroom set up. The list is long and points to the need for high quality long-term training and support for teachers. But he suggests a number of policy issues which need to be addressed for the successful implementation of co-operative learning:

- There should be support and encouragement from top levels of administration, and teacher involvement in planning and implementation.
- There should be adequate funding for training, support and materials.
- Support groups should be established.
- There should be a risk free environment for teachers to adopt co-operative learning.
- Co-operative learning should be modelled in establishment decision- making.
- A co-operative learning library should be set up with appropriate materials.
- Students should be involved through a student council.
- TEIs should adopt co-operative learning so that it can be modelled for student teachers.
- Curriculum and instructional strategies should be developed in tandem.

There can be no doubt that while co-operative learning is adopted piecemeal across the country it will have limited impact. I have mentioned North Lanarkshire Education Department's co-ordinated approach and the efforts they are making to support local authority wide implementation of co-operative learning. These are worthy efforts as part of their overall raising achievement policy and their implementation of A Curriculum for Excellence. The Future Learning and Teaching (FLaT) programme, funded by SEED, has encouraged a bottom-up approach to innovative curriculum design and pedagogy, and the evaluation of the Critical Skills Programme model in a Glasgow cluster was supported by this programme. An extension to that evaluation has funded a subsequent project to follow newly qualified teachers into their probation year to assess the extent to which they use the co-operative learning techniques learned in the PGDE (Primary) course at the University of Glasgow. The evaluation report is due for publication in the autumn of 2006.

In some ways the mixture of bottom-up initiative with top-down support is a recipe for success in terms of lasting change. The top-down support is in place for formative assessment and the impact is substantial. Within the framework of A Curriculum for Excellence, the kind of broad-based co-ordinated support given to formative assessment could also be made available to support the introduction of co-operative learning on wide scale. The research base is as sound as that which informed the AifL programme, the practice is effective, especially in relation to delivering the four key capacities identified in A Curriculum for Excellence, and there is a significant practice base to consider wider evaluation and review. I am convinced that the combination of the three elements: co-operative learning and the Assessment is for Learning initiative with their strong research base, and the framework of A Curriculum for Excellence, would deliver a radically different and more effective climate for learning in our classrooms, with a clear focus on teaching for understanding, empowering autonomous learners, working together and creating a sense of community.

Conclusion

It is clear then that some of the issues that affect student teachers as they consider embarking upon non-traditional teaching strategies also affect newly qualified teachers. The pressure to fit in and conform is, for most of them, a critical factor in the decisions they make about how they will organise learning in their classrooms. So the climate for collaboration and community building needs to extend to the school itself if we are to grant new teachers the freedom and support to work in innovative and stimulating ways with children. As change creeps into Scottish primary schools, recent experience indicates that students and new teachers may find an increasingly accommodating environment within which to experiment with new approaches to teaching.

The issues to be addressed are similar for all three sections of the teaching profession whether they are student teachers, newly qualified teachers or experienced teachers. First of all, teachers need to have a sound understanding of the theory, research base and practice associated with this approach to teaching and learning. Secondly, they need to have the time to assimilate the pedagogy and make sense of it in relation to their own professional beliefs and values. The level of support within the school, the local authority and nationally are key determinants of the ease with which innovative practice will be implemented and sustained. The support mechanisms already mentioned are crucial pieces of the jigsaw if there is to be any long-term impact. I believe that, given the current policy context, we are well placed in Scotland to make some progress on these bigger picture issues around training and support. I hope that this modest contribution to the debate will encourage others to take seriously the opportunity we have before us to make significant change to the way we organise learning in Scottish primary schools.

But individuals can also make a difference. We know from our own experience as learners, when our teachers were brave enough to reach out and make real connections with us. Palmer urges us to have the courage to teach from the heart like those teachers we remember, teachers responsible for

> generations of students whose lives have been transformed by people who had the courage to teach – the courage to teach from the most truthful places in the landscape of self and world, the courage to invite students to discover, explore, and inhabit those places in the living of their own lives.

> (Palmer, 1998, p. 183)

They were people who cared, who brought out the best in us and created the conditions where we felt valued and able to learn. I believe children deserve nothing less and that co-operative learning can help make it happen.

Appendix

DECIDING IF THIS APPROACH IS FOR YOU

Because I believe strongly that you need to work out what you believe about learning and teaching and genuinely reflect on your own practice, I suggest you begin with the books which help you to do just that. For me the best are:

O Palmer, P .J. (1998) *The Courage to Teach*, San Francisco: Jossey-Bass

O Covey, S. R. (1998) *The 7 Habits of Highly Effective People*, London: Simon & Schuster

O Brookfield, S. D. (1995) *Becoming a Critically Reflective Teacher,* San Francisco: Jossey-Bass

O Kohn, A. (1996) *Beyond Discipline: from Compliance to Community*, Alexandria, VA: Association for Supervision and Curriculum Development

Co-operative learning

Then if you want to read more about co-operative learning, these are useful sources.

O Johnson, D. W. and Johnson, R. T.

All of the Johnson books referenced in the text are worth reading. For me their model of co-operative learning is the most flexible and the most useful and I have used their ideas extensively. Their emphasis on helping teachers to understand the conceptual model is crucial because if we really understand *why* we are using this instructional strategy, it so much easier to work out *how* to do it. You can access their material online at http://www.co-operation.org/ This link takes you to their Co-operative Learning Centre at the University of Minnesota.

O Baloche, L. A. (1998) *The Co-operative Classroom: Empowering Learning*, London: Prentice-Hall

This book blends some theory at the beginning with lots of practical advice on how to put co-operative learning into practice. Importantly, it asks you to think about why you are doing the activities and how they will improve learning.

○ Jacobs, G. M., Power, M. A. and Inn, L. W. (2002) *The Teacher's Sourcebook for Co-operative Learning*, London: Sage

This is very practical book which really addresses very helpfully the 'how' to organise co-operative learning. It does not go into the 'why'.

○ Kagan, S. (1992) *Co-operative Learning*, San Juan, Capistino: Kagan Co-operative Learning

This an expensive but very useful encyclopedia of all the possible co-operative learning structures you might want to use in your classroom. The Kagan model includes an element of competition between groups, which I don't find helpful, but this is a very comprehensive range of possible structures which can be put into practice.

Staff development

In terms of training, the most influential experiences for me have been through North Lanarkshire's Co-operative Learning Academies, although I was first introduced to this methodology in the Critical Skills Programme. I have no doubt that you need to experience co-operative learning to truly appreciate its power. The course handbooks and materials from the courses have been very helpful in practical terms, but the experience of working collaboratively over a number of days with highly skilled trainers was the most illuminating.

REFERENCES

Antil, L. R., Jenkins, J. R., Wayne, S. K., Vadasy, P. F. (1998) 'Cooperative learning: prevalence, conceptions, and the relation between theory and practice', *American Educational Research Journal*, Vol. 35, No. 3, pp. 419–54

Assessment Is for Learning (2002) (online). Available from URL: www.ltscotland.com/ assess/ (accessed 5 July 2006)

Baloche, L. A. (1998) *The Co-operative Classroom: Empowering Learning*, London: Prentice-Hall

Baron, S., Martin, M., McConnell, F., McPhee, A., McQueen, I. and Wilkinson, E. (2004) *Evaluation of Aspects of the Critical Skills Project in Glasgow*, Edinburgh: SEED

Bayne, R. (1995) *The Myers-Briggs Type Indicator: A Critical Review and Practical Guide*, London: Chapman & Hall

Black, P. and Wiliam, D. (1998a) 'Assessment and classroom learning', *Assessment in Education*, Vol. 5, No. 1, pp. 7–74

Black, P. and Wiliam, D. (1998b) *Inside the Black Box: Raising Standards through Classroom Assessment*, London: King's College

Black, P. J. (1993) 'Formative and summative assessment by teachers', *Studies in Science Education*, Vol. 21, pp. 49–97

Boud, D. and Miller, N. (1996) *Working with Experience: Animating Learning,* London: Routledge

Brookfield, S. D. (1995) *Becoming a Critically Reflective Teacher*, San Francisco: Jossey-Bass

Bubb, S. (2001) *A Newly Qualified Teacher's Manual*. London: Fulton

Carnell, E. and Lodge. C. (2002) *Supporting Effective Learning*, London: Paul Chapman

Central Advisory Council for Education (1967) *Children and their Primary Schools: A Report of the Central Advisory Council for Education (England)* (The Plowden Report), London: HMSO

Clarke, S. (2001) *Unlocking Formative Assessment*, London: Hodder and Stoughton

Clarke, S. (2003) *Enriching Feedback in the Primary Classroom*, London: Hodder Murray

Clarke, S. (2005) *Formative Assessment in Action*, London: Hodder Murray

Condie, R., Livingston, K. and Seagreaves, L. (2005) *The Assessment is for Learning Programme: An Evaluation*, Edinburgh: SEED

Covey, S. R. (1992) *The 7 Habits of Highly Effective People*. London: Simon & Schuster

Craigen, J. and Ward, C. (1999) *Co-operative Learning: A Resource Booklet*, Ontario: Durham School District Board

Craigen, J. and Ward, C. (2004) *What's this got to do with Anything? A Collection of Group/ Class Builders and Energizers*, Ontario: Durham School District Board

Critical Skills Programme (1997) *Level I Coaching Kit*, Burnsville, NC: Antioch University

Day, C. (2004) *A Passion for Teaching*, London: Routledge Falmer

Deutsch, M. (1949) 'A theory of cooperation and competition on group process', *Human Relations,* Vol. 2, No. 2, pp. 129–52

Dewey, J (1963) *Education and Experience*, New York: Collier Books

Draper, J., Fraser, H. and Taylor, W. (1992) *A Study of Probationer Teachers*, Edinburgh: SOED

Draper, J., O'Brien, J. and Christie, F. (2004) 'First impressions: the new teacher induction arrangements in Scotland', *Journal of In-Service Education*, Vol. 30, No. 2, pp. 201–24

Draper, J., and O'Brien, J. (2006) *Induction: Fostering Career Development at All Stages*. Edinburgh: Dunedin Academic Press.

Emmer, E. T. and Gerwels, M. C. (2002) 'Cooperative learning in elementary classrooms: teaching practices and lesson characteristics', *The Elementary School Journal*, Vol. 103, No. 1, pp. 75–91

Emig, J. (1977) 'Writing as a mode of learning', *College Composition and Communication*, Vol. 28, No. 2, p. 122

Entwistle, N. (1988) *Styles of Learning and Teaching*, London: Wiley

Eraut, M. (1994) *Developing Professional Knowledge and Competence*, London: Falmer Press

Feiman-Nemser, S. (2001) 'Helping novices to teach: lessons from an exemplary support teacher', *Journal of Teacher Education*, Vol. 52, No. 1, pp. 17–30

Fullan, M. (2001) *The New Meaning of Educational Change*, London: Routledge Falmer

Gardner, H. (1983) *Frames of Mind*, New York: Basic Books

Gardner, H. (1999) *Intelligence Reframed: Multiple Intelligences for the 21st Century*, New York: Basic Books

Gilborn, D. and Youdell, D. (2001) 'The New IQism: Intelligence, "Ability" and the Rationing of Education', in Demaine, J. (ed.) (2001) *Sociology of Education Today*, Basingstoke: Palgrave

Gillen, T. (1992) *Assertiveness for Managers*, Aldershot: Gower

Gillies, R. (2000) 'The maintenance of cooperative and helping behaviours in cooperative groups', *British Journal of Educational Psychology*, Vol. 70, No. 1, pp. 97–111

Gillies, R. and Ashman, A. (eds) (2003) *Co-operative Learning: the Social and Intellectual Outcomes of Learning in Groups*, London: Routledge Falmer

Glasgow City Council Education Department (2003) 'Coaching in Context' (online). Available from URL: www.nationalpriorities.org.uk/EAs/EA_GetEA.php?EA=Glasgow (accessed 3 August 2006)

Goleman, D. (1996) *Emotional Intelligence*, London: Bloomsbury

Griffith, R. (2000) *National Curriculum: National Disaster*, London: Routledge Falmer

Hallam, S., Kirton, A., Peffers, J., Robertson, P. and Stobart, G. (2004) 'Project 1 of the Assessment is for Learning development programme: support for professional practice in formative assessment' (online). Available from URL: www.scotland.gov.uk/publications /2004/10/19947/42988 (accessed 10 July 2006)

Hargreaves, A. and Woods, P. (eds) (1984) *Classrooms and Staffrooms: The Sociology of Teachers and Teaching*, Milton Keynes: Open University Press

Hayes, D. (2001) 'The impact of mentoring and tutoring on student primary teachers' achievements: a case study', *Mentoring and Tutoring*, Vol. 9, No. 1, pp. 5–21

Hayward, L., Priestly, M. and Young, M. (2004) 'Ruffling the calm of the ocean floor: margining practice, policy and research in assessment in Scotland', *Oxford Review of Education*, Vol. 30, No. 3, pp. 397–415

Hoover, L. (1994) 'Reflective writing as a window on preservice teachers' thought processes', *Teaching and Teacher Education*, Vol. 10, No. 1, pp. 83–93

Huling-Austin, L. (1990) 'Teacher induction programs and internships', in Houston, W. R. (ed.) (1990) *Handbook of Research on Teacher Education*, New York: Macmillan

Hutchison, C. and Hayward, L. (2005) 'The journey so far: assessment for learning in Scotland', *The Curriculum Journal*, Vol. 16, No. 2, pp. 225–48

Johnson, D. W. and Johnson, F. (1991) *Joining Together: Group Theory and Group Skills* (4th edn), Englewood Cliffs, NJ: Prentice-Hall

Johnson, D. W. and Johnson, R. T. (1989) *Cooperation and Competition: Theory and Practice*, Minnesota: Interaction Book Company

Johnson, D. W. and Johnson, R. T. (1993) *Circles of Learning – Cooperation in the Classroom*, Minnesota: Interaction Book Company

Johnson, D. W. and Johnson, R. T. (1999) *Learning Together and Alone: Cooperation, Competition, and Individualization* (5th edn), Englewood Cliffs, NJ: Prentice-Hall

Johnson, D. W., Johnson, R. T. and Stanne, M. B. (2000) 'Cooperative learning methods: a meta analysis' (online). Available from URL: www.co-operation.org/pages/cl-methods. html (accessed 21 July 2006)

Joyce, B. and Showers, B. (1988) *Student Achievement through Staff Development*, New York: Longman

Kagan, S. (1992) *Co-operative Learning*, San Juan Capistrano: Kagan Co-operative Learning

Kohn, A. (1992) 'Resistance to co-operative learning: making sense of its deletion and dilution', *Journal of Education*, Vol. 174, No. 2, pp. 38–57

Kohn, A. (1996) *Beyond Discipline: from Compliance to Community*, Alexandria, VA: Association for Supervision and Curriculum Development

Kohn, A. (1999) *Punished by Rewards: The Trouble with Gold Stars, Incentive Plans, A's, Praise, and Other Bribes*, Boston: Houghton Mifflin

Kolb, D. A. (1984) *Experiential Learning*, Englewood Cliffs, NJ: Prentice-Hall

Krol, K., Veenman, S. and Voeten, M. (2001) 'Toward a more cooperative classroom: observation of teachers' instructional behaviours', *Journal of Classroom Interaction*, Vol. 37, No. 2, pp. 37–46

Lewin, K. (1935) *A Dynamic Theory of Personality*, New York: McGraw-Hill

Lopata, C., Miller, K. and Miller, R. (2003) 'Survey of actual and preferred use of cooperative learning among exemplar teachers', *The Journal of Educational Research*, Vol. 96, No. 4, pp. 232–9

Lortie, D. (1975) *Schoolteacher: A Sociological Study*, Chicago: University of Chicago Press

Mahoney, P., Menter, I. and Hextall, I. (2004) 'The emotional impact of performance-related pay on teachers in England', *British Educational Research Journal*, Vol. 30, No. 3, pp. 435–56

Martin, M. (2005) 'Reflection in teacher education: how can it be supported?', *Educational Action Research*, Vol. 13, No. 4, pp. 525–41

Martin, M. and Rippon, J. (2003) 'Teacher induction: personal intelligence and the mentoring relationship', *Journal of In-Service Education*, Vol. 29, No. 1, pp. 141–62

Martin, M. and Rippon, J. (2005) 'Everything's fine: the experience of teacher induction', *Journal of In-Service Education*, Vol. 31, No. 3, pp. 527–44

McLaughlin, M. W. and Marsh, D. D. (1978) 'Staff development and school change', *Teachers College Record*, Vol. 80, No. 1, pp. 69–94

Moon, J. (1999) *Learning Journals: A Handbook for Academics, Students and Professional Development*, London: Kogan Page

Moon, J. (2004) *A Handbook of Reflective and Experiential Learning: Theory and Practice*, London: Routledge Falmer

Mosley, J. (1998) *Quality Circle Time in the Primary Classroom*, Wisbech: Learning Development Aids

Nias, J. (1989) *Primary Teachers Talking*, London: Routledge

Nias, J., Southworth, G. and Yeomans, R. (1989) *Staff Relationships in the Primary School*, London: Cassell

Osborne, M., McNess, E., Broadfoot, P. with Pollard, A. and Triggs, P. (2000) *What Teachers Do: Changing Policy and Practice in Primary Education*, London: Continuum

Palmer, P. J. (1998) *The Courage to Teach*, San Francisco: Jossey-Bass

Paterson, L. (2003) *Scottish Education in the Twentieth Century*, Edinburgh: Edinburgh University Press

Panitz, T. (2000) 'Why more teachers do not use collaborative learning techniques' (online). Available from URL: www.capecodnet/~tpantiz/tedspage/tedsarticels/whyfewclusers.

htm (accessed 14 July 2006)

Perkins, D. (1992) *Smart Schools: Better Thinking and Learning for Every Child*, London: Free Press

Perkins, D. and Blythe, T. (1994) 'Putting understanding up front', *Educational Leadership*, Vol. 51, No. 5. pp. 4–7

Piaget, J. (1932) *The Moral Judgement of the Child*, London: Routledge and Kegan Paul

Reeves, J., Morris, B., Turner, E. and Forde, C. (2001) 'Exploring the impact of continuing professional development in the context of the Scottish qualification for headship', *Journal of In-Service Education*, Vol. 27, No. 2, pp. 203–33

Richardson, V. (1997) *Constructivist Teacher Education: Building New Understandings*, London: Falmer Press

Rippon, J. and Martin, M. (2003) 'Supporting induction: relationships count', *Mentoring and Tutoring*, Vol. 11, No. 2, pp. 211–16

Rippon, J. and Martin, M. (2006a) 'Call me teacher', *Teachers and Teaching*, Vol. 12, No. 3, pp. 305–24

Rippon, J. and Martin, M. (2006b) 'What makes a good induction supporter?', *Teaching and Teacher Education*, Vol. 22, No. 1, pp. 84–99

Salovey, P. and Mayer, J. D. (1990) 'Emotional intelligence', *Imagination, Cognition and Personality*, Vol. 9, pp. 185–211

Scottish Consultative Council on the Curriculum (1996) *Teaching for Effective Learning*, Dundee: SCCC

Scottish Executive Education Department (1999) *Review of Assessment in Pre-School and 5-14*, Edinburgh: SEED

Scottish Executive Education Department (2000) www.nationalpriorities.org.uk (accessed 30 June 2006)

Scottish Executive Education Department (2004) *A Curriculum for Excellence*, Edinburgh: SEED

Scottish Executive Education Department (2005) *Review of Initial Teacher Education Stage 2: Ministerial Response*, Edinburgh: SEED

Scottish Office Education Department (1965) *Primary Education in Scotland* S(the Primary Memorandum), Edinburgh: HMSO

Scottish Office Education Department (1991) *Guidelines on Assessment 5–14*, Edinburgh: SOED

Scottish Office Education Department (1992) Circular 12/92, Edinburgh: SOED

Scottish Office Education Department (1998) *The Early Intervention Programme: Raising Standards In Literacy And Numeracy*, Edinburgh: SOED

Scottish Teachers for a New Era (online). Available from URL: www.abdn.ac.uk/stne/ (accessed 10 December 2006)

Sergiovanni, T. J. (1994) *Building Community in Schools*, San Francisco: Jossey-Bass

Simpson, M. (2003) 'Diagnostic and formative assessment in the Scottish classroom', in Bryce, T. G. K. and Humes, W. M. (eds) (2003) *Scottish Education Second Edition: Post Devolution*, Edinburgh: Edinburgh University Press, pp. 721–30

Slavin, R. E. (1995) *Cooperative Learning: Theory, Research and Practice*, Boston: Allyn and Bacon

Smith, I. (2001) *Can Schools get beyond Discipline?* Glasgow: Learning Unlimited

Smith, I. (2005) *Different in Similar Ways*, Edinburgh: The Stationery Office

Smith, I. (2006) *Teaching for Understanding – from Coverage to Comprehension*, Edinburgh: The Stationery Office

Teachers for a New Era (online). Available from URL: www.teachersforanewera.org/index. cfm?fuseaction=home.aboutTNE (accessed 10 December 2006)

Tickle, L. (2000). *Teacher Induction: The Way Ahead*, Buckingham: Open University Press

Veenman, S., Kenter, B. and Post, K. (2000) 'Cooperative learning in Dutch primary classrooms', *Educational Studies*, Vol. 26, No. 3, pp. 281–302

Veenman, S., van Benthum, N., Bootsma, D., van Dieren, J. and van der Kemp, N. (2002) 'Cooperative learning in Dutch Primary classrooms', *Teaching and Teacher Education*, 18, pp. 87–103

Vygotsky, L. S. (1978) *Mind in Society: The Development of Higher Psychological Processes*, Cambridge, Mass.: Harvard University Press

Ward, H. (2004) ' "Cowed" teachers lack confidence' (online). Available from URL: www. tes.co.uk/search/?story/_id=397956 (accessed 10 December 2006)

Weatherley, C. (2000) *Leading the Learning School*, Stafford: Network Educational Press

Wiliam, D. and Thompson, M. (2006) 'Integrating assessment with learning: what will it take to make it work?' (online). Available from URL: www.dylanwiliam.net (accessed 10 December 2006)

Wittrock, M. C. (1978) (ed.) *Learning and Instruction*, Berkeley, Ca.: McCutchan Pub. Corp.

Wragg, E. C., Wragg, C. and Chamberlain, R. (2004) *Jersey Critical Skills Programme – An Evaluation*, States of Jersey: Department for Education, Sport and Culture

Index

ability groupings 14–15
accountability: group work 66; individual
48–9, 66; teachers 5, 25, 27
Ahlberg, Allan 15
Antil, L. R. 24, 64
Ashman, A. 24
assessment: formative vii, 6, 7, 20, 21, 54,
76; staff development 8–9; summative 6;
see also self-assessment
Assessment Development Programme 6
Assessment is for Learning (2002) 4, 5–9,
12, 21, 62, 72

Baloche, L. A. 40–2, 49, 50, 78
Baron, S. 24, 68–9
base teams 44
belonging, sense of 46
Black, P. 6, 8, 19–21, 25
Blythe, T. 17
Boud, D. 16
brainstorm 51
brainstorm carousel 51–2
Brookfield, S. D. 29, 32, 33, 34, 36–7, 42,
55, 78

Canadian studies 22, 69
Carnell, E. 18, 19
child-centred approaches 1–2, 71
children: development 1–2; experiences
42–4; feedback 33–4, 55–6; interactions
with each other 19–20; labelled 3,
14–15; relations with teachers 9, 30, 31,
40–2, 54, 71
Circle Time 40, 45–6
Clarke, S. 21
class bonding 45–6
co-constructivism 19
collaborative learning environment 61
collaborative working 19, 44–5, 61; see
also co-operative learning; group work
competition 48, 79
compliance 56–8
Condie, R. 9
conformity 63–4
connectedness 41, 43–4
constructivism 17–19, 24
continuing professional development

59–60, 64–9
control mechanisms 56–8
co-operative learning 22–4, 42; assessment
vii, 54; feedback 54; group identity 46;
group management 50–1; implementation
64–5, 74–6; learning environment 24–6;
models and methods 51–3, 65–6; reading
resources 78–9; resistance to 71, 74;
skills learned 53; training and support in
59–60, 66–7, 69–74, 75–6; whole school
involvement 68
Co-operative Learning Co-ordinator 73
Covey, S. R. 27–8, 29, 31, 73, 78
Craigen, J. 13, 45
critical reflection 31, 32–8
Critical Skills Programme 24, 42, 65, 68–9,
72, 75
A Curriculum for Excellence (SEED)
75; depth/breadth of learning 26; key
capacities 4–5, 76; pedagogical change
22; reflection 12; student teachers 62;
teacher education 60; transformational
learning 16
curriculum-centred approaches 2–3, 25

Day, C. 31
Deutsch, M. 23
Devolved School Management 2
Dewey, John 16, 26, 43
discussions, effective 20

Early Intervention 73
Education (Scotland) Act (1981) 2
Emig, J. 74
Emmer, E. T. 65
emotional intelligence 30, 31–2
enculturation process 63–4
English national curriculum 2, 3
Eraut, M. 35, 67
evaluation: see assessment; feedback
experiences, sharing 18–19, 33–5, 43
expert groups 52

feedback 7; children 33–4, 49, 55–6; co-
operative learning 54; performance 55;
success criteria 20; see also assessment
5-12 guidelines on Mathematics and